PENGUIN MODERN CLASSICS
Stars from Another Sky

SAADAT HASAN MANTO, the most widely read and the most controversial short-story writer in Urdu, was born on 11 May 1912 at Samrala in Punjab's Ludhiana district. In a literary, journalistic, radio-scripting and film-writing career spread over more than two decades, he produced twenty-two collections of short stories, one novel, five collections of radio plays, three collections of essays, two collections of personal sketches and many scripts for films. He was tried for obscenity half a dozen times, thrice before and thrice after independence. Some of Manto's greatest works were produced in the last seven years of his life, a time of great financial and emotional hardship for him. He died several months short of his forty-third birthday, in January 1955, in Lahore.

KHALID HASAN, journalist, writer and translator, was born in Srinagar, Kashmir. He has translated most of Saadat Hasan Manto's work. He has also translated the stories of Ghulam Abbas and the poetry of Faiz Ahmed Faiz. Khalid Hasan's own publications include *Scorecard, Give Us Back Our Onions, The Umpire Strikes Back, Private View* and *Rearview Mirror*. He lived in Washington and was US correspondent of *Daily Times* and the *Friday Times*, Lahore. Khalid Hasan passed away in February 2009.

JERRY PINTO has been reading film journalism of all kinds from the first time he went to a barber shop alone. He lives and works in Mumbai, not far from where Manto visited Sitara Devi and discovered the rejuvenating effects of custard. He is the author of *Helen: Life and Times of an H-Bomb* which won the National Award for the Best Book on Cinema.

SAADAT HASAN MANTO

Stars from Another Sky
THE BOMBAY FILM WORLD
OF THE 1940s

Translated from the Urdu by Khalid Hasan
With an Introduction by Jerry Pinto

PENGUIN BOOKS
An imprint of Penguin Random House

PENGUIN BOOKS

USA | Canada | UK | Ireland | Australia
New Zealand | India | South Africa | China | Singapore

Penguin Books is part of the Penguin Random House group of companies
whose addresses can be found at global.penguinrandomhouse.com

Published by Penguin Random House India Pvt. Ltd
4th Floor, Capital Tower 1, MG Road,
Gurugram 122 002, Haryana, India

Penguin
Random House
India

First published in English by Penguin Books India 1998
First published in Penguin Modern Classics 2010

Translation copyright © Khalid Hasan 1998, 2010
Introduction copyright © Jerry Pinto 2010

10 9 8 7 6 5 4 3 2

ISBN 9780143415367

Typeset in Sabon by R. Ajith Kumar, New Delhi

Printed at Repro India Limited

www.penguin.co.in

MIX
Paper from
responsible sources
FSC® C047271

This is a legitimate digitally printed version of the book and therefore might not
have certain extra finishing on the cover.

In memory of Saadat Hasan Manto

*Dedicated to Bombay, his beloved city, and to all the
wonderful men and women of the cinema of the 1940s
who made it what it was*

CONTENTS

INTRODUCTION

Manto?

The same Saadat Hasan Manto who is now an icon for all left-leaning, secular liberals?

That Manto, a film journalist? The Manto of 'Toba Tek Singh'?

Stars from Another Sky is indeed a collection of the film journalism of that very Manto. But although he did write about Bollywood, though he did record that Pran was Kuldip Kaur's male mistress, that Naseem always wore pastel colours, it is very soon quite clear that he was no ordinary film journalist.

He was already a famous writer and well known enough for the editor of the magazine for which these pieces were written to allow him to speak so intimately and so personally to the readers. One of the first things one is told when one is setting out to be a journalist is that the first person singular is not welcome. Manto uses it liberally but with telling effect. He is not the outsider, watching the curious antics of the city's beautiful and bizarre people. He is one of them; he is implicated and he takes his place with a curious mixture of pride and self-revelation. He is proud of his long friendship with Ashok Kumar and tells us of how he dismissed the story of K. Asif's *Phool* as 'trash'. But he also tells us about how he felt burnt to a cinder when Nur Jehan refused to sing for his guests. When Manto takes some out-of-town guests to meet Nargis, he grows bored with the artificial conversation. When Rafiq Ghaznavi addresses him familiarly, he feels the flick of the lash on his exposed ego.

But then Manto tells us again and again of his role in the creation of that world. He translated film pamphlets into Urdu, he wrote film scripts for several studios and even appeared in front of the camera despite acute stage fright. His involvement with cinema did not allow him the highbrowed tone of the critic. In fact, these pieces often do not deal very much with the work of the person who is being profiled. In 'Rafiq Ghaznavi: The Ladies' Man', there is a single mention of a film song—the chorus for *Sikander* that runs *Zindagi hai pyar se, pyar se bitai ja*—in the entire piece. In the story on Nur Jehan, he does not mention a single film song and the only performance he mentions is in passing.

But that's not the only anomaly. Consider the names of the people Manto chooses to profile. Only three of them would be recognizable to most film fans today: Ashok Kumar, Nargis and Nur Jehan. Does anyone remember V.H. Desai, described here as a man who could not tell the difference between peeshap and Peshawar? Who remembers Neena alias Shahida Abdullah, the Inscrutable Housewife who was launched by her lover, W.Z. Ahmed, who stole her from her husband? Similarly, Paro Devi, the courtesan from Meerut, seems to have had very little to commend her. During the shooting of *Shikari*, she was wooden in front of the camera and 'would raise her eyebrows like professional dancing girls as if … quoting a price for her services' but this did not stop Manto from writing about her. It is as if Manto was not writing about the film world, no, not even about film stars from another sky; he was writing about himself.

One of the old saws of journalism is that one reveals a huge amount about oneself when one writes about others. Anyone working on a Manto biography would find a mother lode of information here. Manto was a man with many friends, it would seem, and they were drawn from all walks of life, including a ruffian by the name of Meeda Mota and a dentist, Giani Aror Singh, who has a non-speaking role. One way to read this could be to see it as notes towards an autobiography, a lateral autobiography told by a man who spoke in parentheses all his life.

He can display amazing tact: the entire piece on Nargis is written with not a single mention of Raj Kapoor. We are told of how a certain mannerism was used in *Barsaat*; that's it. And yet he can be astonishingly lewd:

One day I went to the Imperial Film Company to meet Seth Ardeshir Irani, the owner. As I walked into his room through the swing door, I found him pumping one of Sheedan's breasts as if it were one of those old-fashioned car horns.

Could this be because Nargis was a star and Sheedan, only the younger sister of Zohra Mirza, who had not made much impact on the box office in her first film in Lahore, *Beli*? One doubts it. On the whole, one gets the sense of someone who is saying whatever comes to mind, a journalistic flow of consciousness, a narrative without too much strategy.

And then one hits something like 'Nawab Kaashmiri: An Actor's Actor'. The beginning of the piece is so startlingly different from everything that has gone before that one is almost puzzled by it. It seems like one of those standard eulogies that Hindi film journalists still write. He explains how Nawab Kaashmiri would not take a role until he had thought about it for days. He shows him to be dedicated enough to his work to have all his teeth extracted to play a convincing man. He talks of Kaashmiri drinking with pickpockets in order to get ready to play one. He tells us how Premankur Atorthy, Kaashmiri's director in the first version of *Yahudi ki Ladki*, said that the world would not see an actor like Nawab again.

And then in the last few paragraphs, he lets fly. The piece works itself into a crescendo, ending with a savage: 'May God keep him in hell where he would be happier'.

Here is another way to read *Stars from Another Sky*. Think of it as a Midaq Alley of Bollywood, in which characters come and go from story to story. We meet Ashok Kumar as a man who was far too shy to ever to do anything about the numerous women who threw themselves at him. We are tantalized by a story:

Another actress plucked up her courage and invited him to her home. Once he was there she told him tenderly how much she loved him. Ashok's reaction was so abrupt that to keep face, she had to assure him she was only testing him and only had sisterly feelings towards him. The amusing thing was that Ashok liked her and would have loved to get her into bed.

Many pages later, we find out who the actress was. (I'm not telling. Find out for yourself.) Ashok Kumar also turns up in the piece on Nargis with Jaddan Bai playing producer; he co-stars with Paro Devi in *Shikari*. In these other chapters, he is referred to charmingly, casually, as Ashok. And when Manto takes the redoubtable Rafiq Ghaznavi to see Naseem, we get this exquisite piece of physical comedy:

> When he came to my room, he began to dance and praise Naseem's beauty. He jumped on a table, dropped to the floor with a thud, swerved and swivelled for some time, then crept under a table, hit his head, re-emerged, stood up and started singing.

In piece after piece, he seems to be intent on belittling his subject. Here is Manto at his most judgmental:

> But the special gift that Rafiq possessed in my view was his utter lack of honour and shame. I would not call him characterless because he was not an ordinary person but an artist.

Of course, he gives you his reasons, and the sexual shenanigans of some of these characters are almost alarming, even for our hardened sensibilities. But just when one is beginning to tire of this, one comes across one of the most beautiful pieces in this collection, on his best friend, Shyam. Once again, Shyam will ring no bells except in the heads of a few film buffs. Although I am no expert on the films of the 1940s and the 1950s, the only film in which I can remember him is Bhagwan Dada's *Albela*.

Shyam does seem to have had some films as lead but it would be safe to say that he has been reclaimed from obscurity by the very real emotion in Manto's piece on him. It begins with a casual admission, almost offhand, that the news of Shyam's death came to Manto when he was in a mental asylum, freeing himself from the fog of alcohol. In dense romantic prose, Manto tells us how he had imagined that several members of his family had died during his time there and then the news of Shyam's death arrives. He shares it with an inmate:

'Do you know that a very dear friend of mine has died?'
'Who?' he asked.
'Shyam,' I replied in a tearful voice.
'Here? In the lunatic asylum?'
I did not answer his question. Suddenly, one after another, several images sprang to life in my fevered brain. Shyam smiling, Shyam laughing, Shyam screaming, Shyam full of life, utterly unaware of death and its terrors.

It is easy to see all this as cinematic, you can imagine the shots merging into each other, the background score a dirge played on a sarod, perhaps. In the realm of the Romantic, everything is permissible, and an excess of grief is the only validation that can be offered to friendship. Even the admission of being in a lunatic asylum sits well with the notion of the despairing artist driven to the fringes of society. Manto himself enters a special claim for the artist as we have seen above in how he says Ghaznavi is not characterless because he was 'not an ordinary person but an artist', thereby claiming moral latitude for the creative person.

But even accounting for these cultural underpinnings, you can see how much Manto cared for Shyam. When the latter comes to Lahore, on the wings of success, Manto tries to visit him. Shyam is himself, happy, carefree, laughing, boisterous. But there is little room in the life of a celebrity for an old friend, and Manto finds himself without purchase in the hotel room to which he has been summoned.

And then he recounts the dream he had:

> I fought with Shyam several times. In the morning when
> the milkman came, I was saying with hollow anger, 'You
> scoundrel, you are mean, you are disgraceful … you are a
> Hindu.' I woke up and felt as if the greatest word of abuse
> in the world had left my lips.

Beyond the tinsel and the scandals, beyond the bottles of Deer
whisky from Nasik and Craven A cigarettes, beyond the details
of who was paid how much and what he spent it on, there
are the shadowy outlines of the nations of India and Pakistan
beginning their slow terrible separation from each other. Once
again, Manto tells us of his departure from India, twice, in the
essays on Ashok and then in the one on Shyam. One can only
imagine how these stories were taken by his Pakistani readers,
since there is a great ambivalence that runs underneath this
decision, taken in haste, and as Khalid Hasan tells us in his
Translator's Note, repented at leisure.

Manto may often have felt let down by the world, by the
literary establishment and by the judiciary but even when he
was writing these memoirs, he could not resist taking a few
sideways swipes:

> Personally, I don't know the difference between the Sunni
> and the Shi'a sects. But I do know that when they fight
> each other, they give evidence that they are off their rocker.

Manto's political stances were also uncompromising. He was
anti-capitalism and anti-feudalism although it was difficult
for ideologues to establish what his brand of socialism or
communism was. But when he says that Jaddan Bai 'had no
illusions about rajas and nawabs; she knew that their money
smelt of the blood of the poor', one has the strong suspicion he
is reading his own values on to hers. But he was not without the
ability to look ironically at himself.

I had written the story for a movie called *Keechar* which he had liked because it was based on socialist ideas. I never could understand why the Seth [Nanoobhai Desai], every inch a dirty capitalist, had taken a shine to it.

It is equally difficult to tell from these pieces where Manto stood on the issue of women. The male gaze is deployed time and again, sometimes slyly, sometimes directly. In the piece on Kuldip Kaur, he relishes the pertness of her nose but has Josef Wirsching lamenting that the actress was not well-endowed enough. Manto says that he broke the news to the actor, telling her that her problem could be solved for thirty-five rupees at Whiteway Laidlaw store. He seems to enjoy outing courtesans and the women who got away, pointing them out as the wife of Mr So-and-So of Such-and-Such a company. He can be breathtakingly frank: Nur Jehan's elder sister ran a whorehouse; Paro Devi was a cut above the ordinary bazaar women because she had had the benefit of a better clientele; Babu Rao Patel of *FilmIndia* slaps his secretary on the bottom. All these details are a little startling, specially since they are almost all gratuitous and do not add much to the stories.

But when you read this book, honourable ladies and gentlemen of the jury, I would like to draw your attention to the way the pieces on Nur Jehan and Sitara Devi end.

He has just finished describing Nur Jehan's talent in the most exalted terms. He has described the beauty of her son, Akbar, dancing in a play at Chiefs College, as Radha. He has said that a single note from her could enthral an audience. He has listed her fans, the ordinary people, the drivers and the cooks. To that list, he adds himself:

And, finally, there is Saadat Hasan Manto who cannot stand the sight of her awful brassiere. What beauty she sees in her upturned front bumpers and why Syed Shaukat Hassan Rizvi permits this gross violation of taste, I am unable to say.

Sitara Devi's love affairs are described in great detail. She is no mere woman, according to the evidence Manto adduces, but a maneater. In three paragraphs, three men claim that their fall from grace, their loss of health, their state of being alone and palely loitering, has to do with the danseuse. And then Manto closes:

> In my book, she walks tall. I do not know what she thinks of me but I have always thought of her as a woman who is born once in a hundred years.

One may not agree with Manto, one may have serious misgivings about his politics, one may not feel completely comfortable with his narrative strategies, but he is never less than entertaining. When you have put down this book, you will feel as if a friendly voice, cheerfully malicious and yet vulnerable in its self-revelation, has been stilled. You will miss it.

From Mumbai, the city Manto loved and lost
July 2010

TRANSLATOR'S NOTE

The pieces that make up this book were written by Saadat Hasan Manto between 1948 and 1954. His nostalgia for Bombay, where he lived from 1936 until January 1948, barring a year and a half in Delhi in the early forties, intensified with time. Till his tragic and early death at the age of 43 in Lahore in 1955, he never really overcame the sense of loss he felt about the city that he had loved and left.

His life in Lahore where he came to live—his wife Safia and his infant daughters were already there—was hard. The movie industry, as it had been before independence, now lay in ruins. In Bombay, Manto had been among the industry's leading film writers and free of financial pressures. He worked with people who were his close friends, men like Ashok Kumar, S. Mukherjee and Savak Vacha. His best friend Shyam also lived in Bombay. That was his world and he had turned his back on it because he was deeply disturbed by the growing religious hatred which he felt was raising its ugly head even in what was once a secular industry. He left Bombay on an impulse and kept wondering for the rest of his days if he had made the right decision.

In Lahore, except for one film which flopped badly at the box office, he did not get any work. Most writers subsisted on their writings for radio but Manto was placed on the banned list. The list was never officially acknowledged but was maintained all the same. What money he made was either through token royalties from his books or newspaper and magazine writings. Almost all the pieces which appear in this book were written for *Daily Afaq*, an Urdu newspaper from Lahore, and *Director*, a popular film monthly, edited by Chaudhri Fazle Haq. So hard up was Manto, that he was known to sometimes walk in, ask for some paper, sit down in a corner, produce a piece in an hour or so, ask to be paid and walk out. Even when he had no money, which was most of the time, he would have a tonga waiting for him on the street while he did his rounds. Many of the tongawalas of Lahore knew him and would not insist on being paid if he told them that he was a bit short of cash that day. Whenever he came by any, he would pay them generously.

Lack of work and ill health notwithstanding, it was in Lahore during the last seven years of his life that Manto produced some of the greatest short stories written in any language, especially his masterpieces about the holocaust at the time of the partition of India. One of these, *Thanda Gosht*,[1] was declared obscene by the Punjab government, and he was tried and convicted, but the judgment of the lower court was later set aside in appeal. He recalled that period in a postscript to his book *Ganjay Farishtay* where most of the pieces that make up this collection first appeared in book form:

> I felt utterly lost. I wasn't sure what I should do. Should I stop writing altogether, or should I write recklessly, unconcerned with its consequences? A strange listlessness had taken hold of me. Sometimes I wished they would give me a lucrative piece of property so that I would be free of financial worry—and this entire busienss of reading and writing, for some years at least. I dreamt of becoming a different person who would no longer think, preferring to make a living selling contraband goods for profit, or producing illicit liquor. The last possibility I crossed out from my list of alternative lifestyles because I was afraid I would drink half the produce myself. Contraband goods I could not trade because it needed capital and I had none.

While everyone with the slightest influence was busy grabbing rich properties abandoned by the Hindus and the Sikhs who had fled

---

[1] See 'Colder than Ice' in *Kingdom's End: Selected Stories*, translated by Khalid Hasan, Penguin Books India.

across the border to India, Manto got nothing because someone reported to the authorities that he was a 'most dangerous progressive'. Ironically, the Progressive Writers' Movement had already declared him a 'reactionary'. Manto said in a later account that he decided, therefore, to do the only thing he knew, namely write. But the question was what theme or topic was he going to write on. After 'much thought' he came to the conclusion that he would write about the actors and actresses he had known and worked with in Bombay. His first piece published in the newspaper *Afaq* was on Naseem. In Manto's words:

I was happy that I had found a way out and would be safe from teh government's ire and those others who want all writing to be 'clean'. I was wrong. The moment the piece appeared, there was an uproar. The newspaper received scores of letters denouncing the author . . . And when *Murli ki Dhun*, my piece on Shyam, was published, one woman, one Nayyar Bano from Sialkot, wrote a long letter to the editor which made me feel very sorry for her. Here are some excerpts from it:

'I do not consider going to the movies a cardinal sin; nor do I tie a bandage over my eyes when I look at pictures. I have five children and I wish them to grow up to be virtuous. However, since addiction to movies is harmful for character, I have stopped watching them. If I went, so would they. If I stopped them by force, they would wait for the day when they could see them to their hearts' content and with vengeance. I am no child, but there are certain pictures which I do not dare to even look at because if I did so, it would lower me in my own eyes, as if I had violated someone's privacy which would be against good manners. You can turn around and say that such things, such magazines, newspapers and books should be kept out of the reach of children. But that is easier said than done. Can you imagine worrying about locking up the magazine and book you have just been reading, rather than simply leaving it on the table!

'Now please read *Murli ki Dhun* once again and tell me what you think of it. Regardless of how far a person has strayed from the path of virtue or how morally depraved he is, can you imagine him sitting at home, surrounded by his wife and children, and regaling them with the experiences—it does not matter whether they brought him pleasure or whether they caused him disgust—that you have described? He would not do it, no matter how much liquor he had drunk; he would not do it even if he had just emerged from a booze pond. It is just not possible that he would act that way even if he had taken leave of his senses after a couple of swigs. He would never talk such filth, he would never talk about women as if they were mere condiments spicing the main dish. How is it then that whenever the word woman has come to his (Shyam's) lips, it has invariably been prefixed with the epithet *sali*? How, come that when he finds his bed without a woman, he sets it on fire? What service to mankind or public morals is being performed by printing such things in newspapers? People have their homes and families, something which should be kept in mind.

'After all, this world is not the sole property of men that they should wallow in filth and contaminate not only themselves but the innocent as well. Is there no reckoning? Where should one seek refuge? There is no peace at home any longer. What newspapers, magazines and literature are now propagating is perhaps designed to induce parents to raise their children according to such values so that the "positive" results of the exercise should be evident to the world. Perhaps fathers should now teach their sons to splash around in pools of liquor and drag these sali women with them for amusement. Perhaps mothers should now teach their daughters how to lay fresh and clever traps for men. May God protect us! What kind of a world, what kind of a society are we moving towards? Just think about it. I for one can't stop thinking about it and the more I think the more I burn.'

When I read this letter, I swear to God I was deeply affected. I felt pity for Nayyar Bano and her mental condition. I said to myself that I had done a great injustice to this lady and I should make it up to her. But then I thought if I tried to do that in the manner that I wished, she might faint because after all, had she not said she felt lowered in her own eyes by merely looking at a picture, as if she had violated someone's privacy? I did not want her to suffer a shock; she might not survive the experience.

I have no doubt that Nayyar Bano is among those sick and morbid people who should be pitied. In my view, there is only one way to bring them back to health. They should be forced to witness thousands of bottles of liquor being opened, with their corks flying all over the place, and their contents poured into a pool. After that one should put dust in one's hair, pull it out in big tufts, scream every obscenity one knew—and if one couldn't do it oneself, men should be hired for the purpose—read aloud every filthy advertisement for aphrodisiacs and remedies for private male and female ailments from magazines such *Shama*, *Beesween Saddi* and *Roman*, not once but repeatedly. And if this medicine does not result in a cure, then Saadat Hasan Manto should be asked to pick up one of Nayyar Bano's old shoes and beat himself repeatedly on the head with it.

Another correspondent complained that Manto had shown disrespect to the dead by writing about their sexual peccadilloes and exposing their weaknesses instead of drawing a veil over their failings and saying something nice about them. He also complained that Manto's writing was so morally depraved that no 'lady of the house' or children or young girls could be exposed to it. Manto dealt with this correspondent with characteristic relish, in the process laying down his literary manifesto. He wrote:

> If I have committed a sin, then I have committed it consciously. I am assured by the correspondent that in every civilized country and culture, only good words are used to remember those who have passed on, even if they were enemies while they lived. Only their virtues are highlighted; their faults are glossed over or ignored. If that is what indeed happens, then I pronounce a thousand curses on that civilized country and society where every dead person's character and personality is carted off to a laundry so that it can come back all clean and white, ready to be hanged with the placard saying 'of blessed memory'.
>
>   In my reform house, I keep no combs, curlers or shampoos because I do not know how to apply make-up on people. If Agha Hashra[2] was cross-eyed, I have no device with which I could straighten his crooked eye, nor could I make him spout flowers from his mouth instead of the abuse he always did. Nor can I purify the deviant character of Meeraji,[3] in the same way as I have not been able to make my friend Shyam describe self-important women as anything but salis. Every angel who has come to my facility has been barbered thoroughly and in style so that not a single hair was left standing on his head.

Manto's greatest work was produced during these years of hardship and emotional uncertainty. He was devoted to his wife and three daughters, but the thought always gnawed at his heart that he could not keep them in comfort. He worried about the future and what would happen to them after he died.

---

[2] Agha Hashra Kashmiri, the celebrated playwright who was popularly called 'the Indian Shakespeare'.

[3] Urdu poet who worked with Manto at All India Radio, Delhi, in 1940–41 and about whom Manto wrote a very 'Mantoesque' piece in his book *Ganjay Farishtay*.

Then there was his drinking, which, under control and well in hand in Bombay because of the regularity of his life and a set daily work routine, became progressively worse in Lahore, as did the company in which he drank. It was a vicious circle. A younger friend of his from Amritsar, the Punjabi poet Ahmed Rahi, when asked about Manto's death, replied, 'He began to die the moment he left Bombay.'

The happiest years of Manto's life had been spent in the film world of Bombay and it was that time he now re-lived in his writings. The nostalgia of these pieces is deep, and what lends poignancy to them is the unhappy and harsh circumstances under which they were written.

Manto first came to Bombay from his native Amritsar in 1936 to work for the film weekly *Mussawar* owned by Nazir Ludhianwi. He was paid a monthly salary of forty rupees. In 1940, after an argument with Ludhanwi, he resigned. When the legendary film journalist Babu Rao Patel of *FilmIndia* learnt about it, he invited Manto to take over *Karwan*, an Urdu journal he owned. Manto stayed there for seven months only, but by then his career as a screenwriter had begun to take off. He worked for many companies but his happiest and most fruitful years, both creatively and in economic terms, were spent at Bombay Talkies and Filmistan.

Manto wrote in 1950 that for the first three months after his arrival in Pakistan in January 1948, he lived in a daze, unable to collect his thoughts or, in his words, 'to dissociate India from Pakistan and Pakistan from India'. In the end, he said, he stopped thinking about it. 'All day long I would loiter around, without aim or purpose, listen to others but say nothing myself. All conversations appeared to me to be empty and pointless . . . but my aimless loitering did me one good—the dust in my mind started to settle and I began to write, initially only light pieces.'

Manto's love affair with Bombay lasted throughout his life. His powerful memoir about his friend Shyam sums up his feelings about Bombay and the trauma of Partition. 'I found it impossible to decide which of the two countries was now my homeland—India or Pakistan.' In the summer of 1952, in an appendix to one of his finest collections, *Yazid*, he recalled his days in Bombay and wrote about the city he considered the best thing that had ever happened to him:

I want to say that there is great sadness in my heart today, a strange melancholy. Four and a half years ago when I bade farewell to my other home, Bombay, I felt the way I feel today. I was sad at leaving a city where I had spent the hardest, the happiest and the most memorable time of my life. That strip of land which is Bombay had taken me, a footloose young man rejected by his family, into its vast lap and said to me, 'You can be happy here on two paise a day or on hundreds of thousands of rupees. You can also be the world's most miserable person, regardless of what you earn. It will be entirely up to you. Here you can do what you like; no one will speak ill of you. No matter how difficult things become, you will have to deal with them yourself. You and you alone will take every important decision of your life, without interference or help. If you so choose, you may sleep on the street; or it is possible you may find yourself living in a palace. It will be of no consequence to me whatsoever. You may even leave if you like, or stay; but as far as I am concerned, it will make not the least difference. I am where I am and will continue to remain where I am.

I stayed in Bombay for twelve years. And what I am, I am because of those years. Today I find myself living in Pakistan. It is possible that tomorrow I may go to live elsewhere. But wherever I go, I will be what Bombay made me. Wherever I live, I will carry Bombay with me. When I left Bombay, I was sad at leaving it. That was where I had formed the most lasting friendships of my life, friendships of which I am proud. That was where I had got married, where my first child was born, where my second child began the first day of her life. There were times in Bombay when

I did not have enough to eat; and there were times when I was making vast sums of money and living it up. That was the city I loved. That is the city I still love.

This collection invokes and recreates Manto's beloved city and the friends with whom he worked and shared his life for twelve years. The documentary value of these pieces apart, they are also memorable literature, stamped as they are with Saadat Hasan Manto's unique and lively genius.

Washington
February 1997

When Najmul Hasan ran off with Devika Rani, all of Bombay Talkies was in turmoil. The film they were making had gone on the floor and some scenes had already been shot. However, Najmul Hasan had decided to pull the leading lady out of the celluloid world into the real one. The worst affected and the most worried man at Bombay Talkies was Himanshu Rai, Devika Rani's husband and the heart and soul of the company.

S. Mukherjee, Ashok Kumar's brother-in-law, who was to make several hit movies in the years to come, was at that time sound engineer Savak Vacha's assistant. As a fellow Bengali, he felt sorry for Himanshu Rai and wanted to do something to make Devika Rani return. Without saying anything to Rai, he somehow managed to persuade her to come back, which meant that he talked her into abandoning the warm bed of her lover Najmul Hasan in Calcutta and return to Bombay Talkies where her talents had a greater chance of flourishing.

After Devika Rani came back, Mukherjee convinced the still-shaken Himanshu Rai to accept his runaway wife. As for Najmul Hasan, he was left to join the ranks of those who are fated to be deserted by their beloved for less emotional, but weightier political, religious or simply material considerations. As for the scenes he had already done, they were trashed. The question now was: Who was going to be his replacement?

Himanshu Rai was a very hard-working man, a film-maker totally absorbed in his craft, and basically a loner. He had set up Bombay Talkies on the lines of a teaching institution, choosing the village of Malad outside Bombay as the site. He wanted nosy outsiders to be kept out—outsiders like Najmul Hasan. A replacement was needed. Once again, Mukherjee came to the rescue of his emotionally disturbed boss. His wife's brother

1

Ashok Kumar, after taking a bachelor's degree in science and reading law in Calcutta, had joined Bombay Talkies as an unpaid laboratory apprentice. He was quite good-looking and could sing a little. Mukherjee suggested him as Najmul Hasan's replacement. Himanshu Rai, who had spent his entire life experimenting, agreed to look at the young fellow. His German cameraman Wirsching gave Ashok a screen test and showed it to Himanshu Rai, who was satisfied. His German film director, however, had a different opinion, but there was no one who could overrule Himanshu Rai. And so it came to pass that Ashok Kumar Ganguly, who was then no more than twenty-two years old, was chosen to play Devika Rani's leading man.

They made one film, then another, then another, becoming filmdom's inseparable team. Most of their movies were hits. The doll-like Devika Rani and the young and innocent Ashok Kumar looked just right together on the screen. Her artless gestures and girlish ways won the hearts of film-goers who had until then been fed on love's 'heavier', more aggressive screen version. These two delicate, almost fragile-looking young lovers became the toast of India. So popular were they that college girls would pine for Ashok Kumar, while boys would go about wearing long and loose Bengali shirts, sleeves unbuttoned, one of which Ashok Kumar had worn in that famous duet with Devika Rani: *Mein banki chidiya banke bolun re* (I shall become a forest bird and sing from grove to grove).

I had seen some of Ashok's films and as far as acting was concerned, Devika Rani was streets ahead of him. In the beginning, he used to look like someone made of chocolate but as time passed he matured and his style became more assertive.

When he moved from the laboratory to acting, his monthly salary was fixed at seventy-five rupees, a sum he accepted happily. In those days, for a single person living in a far-flung village, which Malad was, it was a lot of money. When his salary was doubled, he was even happier. Not long after, when it was raised to two hundred and fifty rupees, he was very nervous. Recalling that occasion, he said to me, 'My God . . . it was a strange feeling. When I took the money from the studio cashier, my hand was trembling. I did not know where I was going to keep it. I had a place, a tiny house with one bed, two or three chairs and the jungle outside. What would I do if thieves paid me a visit at night? What if they came to know that I had two hundred and fifty rupees? I felt lost . . . I have always been terrified of thefts and robberies, so I finally hid the money under my mattress. That night I had horrible dreams, so next morning I took the money to the post office and deposited it there.'

While Ashok was telling me this story, outside, a film-maker from Calcutta was waiting to see him. The contract was ready but Ashok did not sign it because while he was offering eighty thousand rupees, Ashok was insisting on one lakh. And to think that only some years earlier he had been at a loss to know what to do with two hundred and fifty rupees!

With Ashok doing so well, Mukherjee, an intelligent and highly observant man, also flourished, soon rising to become a big-time producer who made several silver and golden jubilee hits for Bombay Talkies. He established a new style of scripting movies. I, for one, always considered him my teacher.

Ashok's popularity grew each passing day. He seldom ventured out, but wherever he was spotted, he was mobbed. Traffic would come to a stop and often the police would have to use lathis to disperse his fans. He was not too generous with his admirers. In fact, he would get irritated because they wanted to get close to him. He would sometimes react as if someone had abused him. I would often say to him, 'Dadamoni, your reaction is most ridiculous. Instead of being flattered by the attention you receive, you get upset. Can't you understand that these people love you?' However, his brain appeared to me to be devoid of those cells which help you understand unquestioning admiration.

Till the time I left Bombay in 1948, he was totally unfamiliar with love. I am unaware of what changes occurred in him in later years. Hundreds of beautiful women came into his life but he treated them all with the greatest indifference. Temperamentally, he was a rustic. His living style and his food habits also had a touch of rusticity.

Devika Rani tried to have an affair with him but he rebuffed her rather curtly. Another actress once picked up her courage and invited him to her home. Once he was there she told him tenderly how much she loved him. Ashok reacted so brusquely that to save face she had to assure him she was just testing him and had only sisterly feelings towards him. The amusing thing was that Ashok liked her and would have loved to get her into bed. She always wore a washed and scrubbed look, which Ashok found irresistible. When she told him that he was like a brother to her, he felt rather let down.

Ashok was not a professional lover but he liked to watch women, as most men do. He was not even averse to staring at them, especially at those areas of their anatomy that men find attractive. Off and on, he would even discuss these things with his friends. Sometimes he would experience a strong urge to make love to a woman but he would never step forward. Instead he would say something like, 'Yaar Manto . . . I just do not have the courage.' Courage he certainly lacked, which was a good thing for his marriage. I am sure his wife, Shobha, was happy about her husband's timidity, praying that he would never lose it.

I always found it odd that Ashok should be scared of women when hundreds of them were willing to jump if he told them to jump. His mailbag would be full of love letters from thousands of girls, but I do not think he ever read more than a hundred of them in his life. It was his tubercular-looking secretary, de Souza, who would read each letter like a voyeur, only to look even more insubstantial. A few months before Partition, Ashok was in Calcutta for a Chander Shekher film. Huseyn Shaheed Suhrawardy was the chief minister of Bengal at the time. Ashok had been to his home, where they had watched 16-mm home movies. While driving back, two pretty Anglo-Indian girls flagged his car down, wanting a lift. Ashok stopped and they jumped in. However, he had to pay dearly for this vicarious pleasure because one of them not only smoked his cigarettes but also took away his cigarette case. Ashok knew where they lived and often thought of starting something with them, but could never muster up the courage.

Once Ashok was shooting a film in Kolhapur. It was the kind

of rubbish where swords, shields and maces are the actors' mainstay. Ashok's scenes had almost all been done but since he did not like the movie he was not too enthusiastic about shooting the rest of his scenes. He returned to Bombay, where he received message after message begging him to come to Kolhapur. Since a contract was a contract, he did in the end go, but dragged me along, though I was busy writing *Eight Days* for Filmistan. Since Ashok was to produce and direct the movie, I couldn't say no, especially when he said, 'Come, yaar, we can work there in peace.'

But how could there be peace? Word soon went around that Ashok Kumar was in town. Our hotel was now almost constantly surrounded by fans. The manager was a clever man and he would somehow manage to make the crowd go away on one pretext or the other. The diehards, however, were not to be fooled or discouraged and would hang around for hours to see their idol. Ashok's attitude was what it had always been: unfriendly, something that I found irritating.

One evening, we went out for a walk with Ashok suitably 'camouflaged' in dark glasses. He had a walking stick in one hand and the other was on my shoulder so that he could manoeuvre me back and forth in case of emergency. We went into a store, as Ashok wanted some anti-allergy tablets to counter the dirt and dust of Kolhapur. The shopkeeper paid no attention to us and turned around to get the medicine from his cabinet. Then something occurred to him. It was like a delayed bomb.

'Who . . . who are you?' he asked.

'Who am I? I am who I am,' Ashok replied. The store owner looked at him carefully. 'You are Ashok Kumar,' he said.

'Ashok Kumar must be somebody else. Let's go, Manto,' Ashok said.

Then he placed his hand on my shoulder and walked out of the store without buying the medicine. As we were turning towards our hotel, three Maharashtrian girls appeared. They were pretty and their hair was parted in the middle with the parting sprinkled with kumkum. They were also wearing flowers in their hair. One of them had a couple of oranges in her hand and she was the one who noticed Ashok. She began to quiver and said to her friends in a stifled voice, 'Ashok.' As she said it, the oranges fell from her hands. Ashok let go of my shoulder and ran towards the hotel. He was always like that with women.

I first met Ashok at Filmistan, which S. Mukherjee had founded after walking out of Bombay Talkies with his entire team. I had caught glimpses of Ashok Kumar here and there but I only got to know him when I joined the new company. Every actor has two personalities, one that you see on the screen and one as he or she really is. When I saw Ashok for the first time at close quarters, he was quite different from what I had seen of him in the movies. He was quite dark with rough and chubby hands, strong of body and semi-rustic in manner. He was also quite formal but in a tense, uneasy kind of way.

Ashok spoke excellent Urdu. He did try to learn to read and write it, but could never go beyond the first primer. However, he learnt enough to write a line or two in the language. When we were introduced, I said, 'I am very pleased to meet you.' Ashok's reply was self-conscious but well rehearsed. Once a visitor to Filmistan said to Ashok in the most formal Urdu, 'I have a feeling that this most humble servant of yours has in the past had the honour of meeting you.' Ashok's reply, delivered in accented Urdu, contained a huge malapropism, of which he soon became conscious, and he slunk away without saying another word. After I left Bombay to come to Pakistan, he wrote me a letter in broken Urdu asking me to come back but for some reason I did not write back.

My wife, like most women, was among Ashok's admirers. One day I brought him home and as we entered I shouted, 'Safia, come out. Ashok Kumar is here.' Safia was cooking. She finally came out since I kept bugging her. I introduced them. 'This is my wife, Dadamoni, shake hands with her.' They both became self-conscious. I took hold of Ashok's hand. 'Dadamoni'—which in Bengali means older brother—'why are you shying away from shaking hands with my wife?' I said. So he had to shake hands. That day my wife had prepared keema parathas. Ashok liked it so much that he ate three parathas. It was strange that whenever my wife prepared keema parathas, somehow Ashok would always appear. None of us could explain why. I suppose it is fated who will eat what, when and where.

I began to call Ashok 'Dadamoni' because he insisted that I should. 'But what makes you think you are older? I can prove to you that I am older,' I argued. When we worked it out, he turned out to be two months older, so from that day on, I began to call him 'Dadamoni' instead of 'Mr Ganguli'. In any case, I liked the sound of the word 'Dadamoni' because it had the gentle sweetness of Bengali culture. In the beginning, he used to call me 'Mr Manto' but when I began to call him 'Dadamoni' he switched to just 'Manto', a form of address for which I did not really care.

Ashok looked soft on the screen but in real life he was a tough person who exercised regularly. He could hit a door hard enough to crack the wood. He used to box at home and was crazy about shikar. He was capable of doing the most arduous job cheerfully. However, he had no interest in keeping an elegant home. Had he wanted, he could have had the best-furnished home in the city but he never bothered about such things and when he tried, the results were disastrous. He would pick up a brush and paint a perfectly nice chair all blue or turn a fine sofa into a divan by removing its back.

Ashok lived in a seafront house but it wasn't very nice. The salt had eaten through the grill that guarded the windows and it was now badly rusted. The place did not smell very nice. However, none of these things had the least effect on Ashok. His refrigerator was parked on the veranda and his big Alsatian slept against it. His children would be creating a rumpus in the living room and Ashok, quite unmindful of them, would be in the loo, working out which horse would win the next big race. He would also rehearse his lines while sitting in the WC.

Ashok was well versed in astrology, which he had learnt from his father. He had read many books on the subject and when he had time he used to tell the fortunes of his friends. One day he asked me my birth date and after working out something on a paper asked if I was married. 'You know that I am,' I replied.

He was quiet for a while, then said, 'I know, but Manto, tell me something. You have no children so far, have you?' 'Why do you ask?' I wanted to know. He hesitated before saying, 'Well, the first child of those with your combination of stars is a male, but he does not survive.' Ashok did not know that I had lost my son when he was a year old.

Ashok later told me that his first child, a son, was stillborn. He explained that his and my stars were in more or less the same configuration and it was not possible for such people to have their firstborn male child not die. Ashok was a complete believer in astrology as long as the calculations were accurate. 'As you can never get the correct balance if even one paisa is wrongly added, similarly, if you do not work out the stars with absolute accuracy, you will get the most misleading results, which is why you should not rely on these things totally because it is possible that your basic data is wrong,' he once told me.

Ashok would place his racing bets on the basis of astrological calculations. He would spend hours working out the winning horses. However, he would never place more than a hundred rupees on any one horse. He would sometimes win ten rupees or come out even, but he never lost. He backed horses not so much to win as to divert himself. He would always be accompanied to the race course by his lovely wife, Shobha, mother of his three children. A few minutes before the start of the race he would give her money and ask her to place it. She would also be the one who would later queue up at the window to pick up the winnings. Shobha was a housewife with a modest education. Ashok would joke about her being illiterate but they had a happy marriage. Despite their money, Shobha would do most of the housework herself, clad like a true Bengali in a cotton sari with the house keys tied in a big bunch around her waist and hanging by the side. Over drinks in the evening, she would prepare delicacies for us to nibble on. Since I drank more than others, she would tell Ashok, 'Look, do not give Mr Manto too much to drink; otherwise his wife will protest to me.'

Our wives were good friends. Often Shobha would take Safia along when she went shopping. Every shopkeeper knew who she was: wife of the famous actor Ashok Kumar. They would, therefore, produce the most sought-after things for her from under the counter. Bombay men, I should point out, generally speaking, were a soft touch, compared to the women. If you had to get your money from a bank or mail a registered letter or buy a cinema or a train ticket and you were a male, you would have to stand in line for hours. However, if you were a woman, you could do the necessary in a matter of minutes. While Ashok never took advantage of his fame and popularity, some others were not that scrupulous. Raja Mehdi Ali Khan was one such.

He worked for Filmistan, which I had left in between, and at the time of the incident was busy writing a story for director Wali sahib. One day, Ashok's secretary phoned to say that Raja was ill. When I went to look him up, he was in bad shape with a throat so sore that he could hardly talk. He was so weak that he could not get up without help. He had been gargling with salt water and rubbing some balm on his chest but it was not working. I was afraid that he might have diphtheria, so I put him in a car and phoned Ashok, who told me to take him to a doctor friend of his, who confirmed that it was indeed diphtheria. On the advice of the doctor we put him in the infectious diseases hospital, where he was given a number of injections. I phoned Ashok and told him about Raja's illness but he showed little concern. I got angry at his attitude and told him so. 'It is strange that here is this man infected with a most serious disease and there you are, behaving in a totally unconcerned manner. You know he has no one to look after him.'

All Ashok said in reply was, 'We will go look him up this evening.' I got off the phone and went to the hospital. Raja was somewhat better. The doctor had suggested certain injections and I had brought the vials with me. I stayed for some time and came away telling Raja not to worry and to hang in there. In the evening, Ashok picked me up from Wali sahib's office. I was still a bit upset with him but he talked me out of my annoyance. He apologized to Raja, explaining that he would have come earlier except that he had been busy. After some time he left. The next day when I went to the hospital, I found everything transformed.

Raja really looked like a raja. His sheets were bright and clean and the pillows had fresh covers. He had a packet of cigarettes and there were flowers in a vase on the windowsill. He was wearing crisp hospital clothes and reading a newspaper. 'What is all this, Raja?' I asked.

Raja smiled through his thick moustache. 'This is nothing. You wait and watch.'

'What?' I asked.

'I have everything that a man needs. If I stay here for a few more days, I will have a harem going in the next room. God bless my Ashok Kumar . . . but where is he?' He then told me that his changed circumstances were entirely due to Ashok Kumar. The hospital management had found out that Ashok had come to see how he was and since then he had half the nursing staff waiting on him, wanting to know if Ashok really had come, and how close their friendship was, and if he would be coming again, and when.

Raja told everyone that Ashok was his dearest friend and was prepared to lay down his life for his sake. That Ashok even wanted to move into the hospital with him but the doctors would not agree to the arrangement. That he would have come twice a day but he was busy working. However, the good news was that he was due to drop in that evening. It had paid off. In that free hospital, every facility was now Raja's. I was about to leave as the visitors' hour had come to an end when a bunch of girl students from the medical college came in. Raja smiled. 'Khwaja, I don't think this adjoining room will be large enough for the harem,' he said to me with a wink.

Ashok, always a fine actor, could only work at his best if he was teamed up with people he knew well. Films where that had not been the case showed him performing indifferently. With his own team around him, he would come alive. He would advise the technicians and accept advice from them. He would ask people their opinion about his acting, and would play a scene in many different ways before deciding upon the final version. He would listen to others, but once he was involved in work, he hated to be interrupted. Being educated and having spent so many years with an institution like Bombay Talkies, Ashok had come to acquire a basic working knowledge about every department of film-making. He understood the finer points of photography and was well informed about all technical aspects of the business. He had practical knowledge of editing and had studied direction seriously. So when Rai Bahadur Chunilal, one of the leading lights of the industry, asked him to produce a movie for Filmistan, he agreed right away.

Filmistan had just completed its war propaganda movie *Shikari*, and all the members of the company were enjoying a well-earned holiday with their families. One day, Savak Vacha dropped in to see me. 'Saadat,' he said after some small talk, 'write a story for Ganguli.' I could not understand what he meant. I was a Filmistan employee and it was my job to write stories. I did not need a recommendation from Savak to write for Ganguli. Any responsible Filmistan official could have asked me to write a story and I would have started doing so there and then. I later learnt that since Ashok himself was going to produce the movie, he wanted me to make a special effort to write a story that would be unique. We gathered at Savak's nice, well-laid-out flat some days later. It was not clear what kind of a story Ashok wanted. 'Manto, I don't know . . . but it should be something sensational. Remember, it is my first film as a producer,' he said.

We sat there for hours, searching for an idea but couldn't come up with any. At the time, a huge stage was being built at the Brabourne Stadium, very close to where Savak lived, in connection with the diamond jubilee celebrations of the Aga Khan's birthday. I thought that might inspire me to think of something, but nothing came. A fine piece of sculpture in Savak's flat also failed to get my creative juices flowing. I tried to get an idea from one of my earlier stories but still nothing clicked. In the evening, after a long and barren day, we placed our chairs on the terrace and began to drink brandy. Savak was a great aesthete when it came to drinks and he had produced an excellent brandy. One sip and you were in seventh heaven. We could see Churchgate station down below and the street was full of people. The sea lay beyond. Expensive cars, shimmering under the street lights, moved about noiselessly. Suddenly from nowhere, one of those huge, ugly roadrollers appeared. It was an odd sight but it gave me an idea. I thought, if a young and beautiful girl standing in her balcony were to drop a piece of paper from above and vow to marry the man who picked it up, she could well find herself married to the driver of the roadroller rather than the owner of one of those sleek, expensive cars. Anything could happen.

When I told Ashok and Vacha, they seemed greatly amused. We poured ourselves some more brandy and began to speculate and throw up ideas and fictional situations in the air. When we parted, it was with the understanding that a story should be worked out on the idea I had come up with. I wrote a story but, of course, it was different. There was no girl in the balcony and no roadroller. I favoured a tragedy but Ashok wanted the story to have a happy ending with fast action. We all zeroed in on 'the story' now. Finally, it was done. Ashok liked it and we began to shoot. Every single frame was prepared under Ashok's supervision. Few people knew that the entire direction of *Eight Days*, the movie we produced, was the work of Ashok Kumar though D.N. Pai's name appeared as director in the credits. He had not directed even an inch of the movie. At Bombay Talkies the film director was not a prima donna as elsewhere. It was all team effort and when the film was ready for release one member of the team would be credited with its direction. We had adopted the same system at Filmistan. D.N. Pai was a film editor and a good one, so it was decided that he should be mentioned as the director of the film.

It was during the making of *Eight Days* that I realized that Ashok was as good a director as he was an actor. He would take great pains over even the smallest scene. A day before the scene was to be shot, he would go over the screenplay—which I had already gone through one final time—and spend hours in the loo ruminating over it. Oddly, Ashok could only concentrate when he was in the loo.

There were four new faces in the movie: Raja Mehdi Ali Khan, Upinder Nath Ashk, Mohsin Abdullah (husband of the actress

Neena who was publicized as the 'Mystery Woman') and I. It had been decided to give a small role to Mukherjee as well but he copped out at the last moment because I had copped out of his film *Chal Chal Re Naujawan* as I was terrified of the camera. But that was only an excuse. The fact was that he was equally terrified of the camera.

Mukherjee was to have played a shell-shocked soldier. Everything was ready including the uniform, and when he said no Ashok was very upset. The shooting had to remain suspended for several days. Rai Bahadur Chunilal began to get worked up about it. One day Ashok burst into my room, where I was busy rewriting a number of scenes. He picked up my papers, put them aside and said, 'Come, Manto.' I got up because I thought he wanted me to hear one of the new songs in the movie. However, when we ended up on the set, I asked him what was up. 'You are playing the crazy,' he announced. I knew that Mukherjee had said no and Ashok had been unable to find a replacement, but I had never imagined he would pick me out, so I said to him, 'You are out of your mind.' Ashok became serious. 'No, Manto, you have got to do it.' Raja Mehdi Ali Khan and Upendranath Ashk felt the same way. Raja said to me, 'Look, I have been asked to play the husband of Ashok's sister, and I find it very embarrassing to be "married" to my good friend's sister, even if it is only in a movie. So what is odd about your playing a man who has lost his marbles?' In the end, I did play Flight Lieutenant Kirpa Ram, the shell-shocked officer, but only God and I know how terror-stricken I felt in front of the camera.

The film was released and it was a success. The public felt that it was a great comedy, which pleased Ashok and me greatly. We wanted to make another new type of film but fate had other things in mind. Savak Vacha had gone to London soon after we began to shoot *Eight Days* for the treatment of his mother. When he returned, the movie industry was in a crisis. Many companies had gone bankrupt and Bombay Talkies was in bad shape. A few years after the death of her husband, Himanshu Rai, Devika Rani had married a Russian émigré by the name of Svetoslav Roerich. She had also turned her back on movies.

Many efforts had been made to put Bombay Talkies back on track but nothing had succeeded. Savak Vacha with the help of Ashok, now made a last-ditch effort to save the company.

Ashok left Filmistan. In the meanwhile, I had been cabled an offer from Lahore by Moti B. Gidwani to work for him at a salary of one thousand rupees a month. I would have gone but I wanted to wait for Savak. When he returned and took Ashok with him to Bombay Talkies, I went with them. This happened on the eve of Partition. The British were now putting the final touches to the map of the subcontinent so that when the whole thing went up in smoke, they would be able to watch it from a distance. Hindu–Muslim riots had begun, and as wickets fall in cricket matches, so were people dying. There were big fires everywhere.

Savak ran into a number of problems right away when he tried to reorganize Bombay Talkies. A lot of people, almost all of them Hindus, were given the sack as they were found to be redundant. This caused an uproar since their places were mostly filled by Muslims. Apart from me, there was Shahid Latif and his wife, Ismat Chughtai. Then there were Kamal Amrohi, the movie director, Hasrat Lukhnavi, Nazim Panipati and the music director Ghulam Haider. This created great resentment against Savak Vacha and Ashok Kumar among the company's Hindu employees. When I mentioned it to Ashok, he laughed. 'I will tell Vacha to sort those johnnies out,' he said.

This was done but it had the opposite effect. Vacha began to receive hate mail. He was told that if he did not get rid of the Muslims, the studio would be set on fire. He would get very angry when he read the letters. 'These salas say I am in the wrong. Well, if I am in the wrong, then the hell with them! If they set fire to the studio, I will push them all into it.' Ashok was utterly devoid of any communal feelings. They were foreign to his nature. He could not even understand why those people were threatening to set fire to the studio. 'Manto, this is madness . . . it will go away; it is only a matter of time.' However, it never went away, this madness. Instead, as time passed, it became more and more virulent. I felt somehow responsible for all that had happened. Ashok and Vacha were my friends and they would seek my advice because they trusted me and they knew I was sincere. However, my sincerity had begun to atrophy. I used to ask myself how I would face Vacha and Ashok if something bad were to happen to Bombay Talkies.

The religious killings were now at their height. One day Ashok and I were returning from Bombay Talkies. We stopped at his place, where I stayed for several hours, and then he offered to drop me home in the evening. He took a short cut through a Muslim neighbourhood. A wedding procession led by a band was approaching us from the other side of the street. I was horrified. 'Dadamoni, why have you come here?' 'Don't you worry,' he said. He knew what I was thinking. But it failed to calm my nerves. We were in an area that no Hindu would dare enter. And the whole world knew Ashok was a Hindu, a very prominent Hindu at that, whose murder would create shock waves. I could remember neither prayers in Arabic nor an appropriate verse from the Quran. But I was cursing myself and praying in broken words, 'O God, don't let me be dishonoured . . . let no Muslim kill Ashok because if that happens, I will carry that guilt to my grave. I am not the entire Muslim nation. I am only an individual but I do not want the Hindu nation to curse me for ever and ever if something happens to Ashok.'

When the procession reached the car, some people spotted Ashok and began to scream, 'Ashok Kumar . . . Ashok Kumar.' I went cold. Ashok had his hands on the steering wheel and he was very quiet. I was about to scream to the crowd that I was a Muslim and Ashok was taking me home when two young men stepped forward and said, 'Ashok bhai, this street will lead you nowhere. It is best to turn into this side lane.'

Ashok bhai? If Ashok was their brother, then who was I? I looked at my clothes which were homespun cotton . . . had they thought I was another Hindu? Or had they not even noticed me because of Ashok? When we got out of the area, I relaxed and thanked God. Ashok laughed. 'You were nervous for nothing. These people never harm artists.'

A few days later, at a meeting held to discuss a story written by Nazir Ajmeri—which was later filmed as *Majboor*—I made some critical remarks, suggesting changes. Nazir turned to Ashok and Vacha and said, 'You should not let Manto sit in on such meetings. Since he is a story writer himself, he is prejudiced.'

It upset me and I felt that it was time I took a decision. I thought about it for several days but couldn't make up my mind. Then I said to myself, 'Manto bhai, this street will lead you nowhere. It is best to turn into this side lane.'

So I took the side lane that brought me to Pakistan, where I was soon tried for obscenity for writing a story called 'Thanda Gosht'.

V.H. DESAI: GOD'S CLOWN

'Lights on . . . fan off . . . camera ready . . . start, Mr Jagtap!'
    'Started.'
    'Scene thirty-four . . . take one.'
    'Neela Devi, you don't have a thing to worry about. I have also drunk the urine of Peshawar . . .'
    'Cut, cut!'
    The lights came on. V.H. Desai placed the rifle against a prop and with the utmost calm asked Ashok Kumar, 'OK, Mr Ganguli?'
    Ashok, who was about to turn from a red-hot cinder into pure ash, looked at Desai with murderous eyes, controlled his anger with a superhuman effort, brought a forced smile to his face and said, 'Wonderful.' Then he looked at me and said, 'Well, Manto?'
    I embraced Desai. 'Wonderful!'
    All around us on the set, people were having a hard time trying to control their laughter. Desai looked extremely pleased. It was after a long time that he had heard such fulsome praise from me. Earlier, Ashok had instructed me never to show my irritation because this would throw Desai off balance and the entire day would be lost.
    After a few minutes, Desai asked Dixit, the dialogue prompter, 'Next dialogue, Dixit sahib?'
    Ashok, the director of *Eight Days*, the movie we were shooting, now addressed me: 'Manto, I think we should do another take of the last scene.'
    I looked at Desai. 'Desai sahib, what do you say? Let it be an even more wonderful shot.'
    Desai shook his head in a typical Gujarati gesture and replied, 'Go right ahead . . . I am hot.'
    Dattaram shouted, 'Lights on.'

17

The lights came on. Desai picked up the rifle.

Dixit leapt towards Desai, the script in his hand. 'Desai sahib, what about going over the lines once again?'

Desai asked, 'Which lines?'

Dixit answered, 'The same lines that you delivered so wonderfully just now. Let's go over them one more time.'

Desai rested the rifle soldier-like on his shoulder and said with absolute confidence, 'I remember them.'

Dixit looked at me. 'Manto sahib, why don't you hear them?'

I placed my hand on Desai's other shoulder and said in a friendly tone, 'So what are those lines, Desai sahib? . . . Neela Devi, you don't have a thing to worry about. I have also drunk the water of Peshawar.'

Desai adjusted the Peshawari-style turban on his head at a rakish angle and said to Veera, who was playing Neela Devi, 'Neela Devi, you do not have a thing to Peshawar about. I have also drunk your water.'

Veera burst out laughing hysterically. Desai looked worried. 'What happened, Miss Veera?'

Veera, with the loose end of her sari between her teeth to control her laughter, ran off the set. Desai, who now looked positively anxious, asked Dixit, 'What was the matter?'

Dixit turned his face away because he too was having a hard time trying not to laugh. To set Desai's mind at rest, I intervened, 'Nothing serious. It was her cough.'

'Oh!' Desai said, relieved. 'Neela Devi, you do not have a thing to cough about, I have also had Devi's . . .'

Ashok, with clenched fists, was hitting himself in the head. This really had Desai worried. 'What is the matter, Mr Ganguli?'

Ashok hit himself one more time. 'Nothing, I have a headache. So let's do this scene.'

Desai shook his pumpkin-like head. 'Done.'

In a dead voice, Ashok called, 'Camera ready . . . ready, Mr Jagtap?'

'Ready,' came Jagtap's thin voice through his hand-held hailer. 'Start.'

The camera began rolling. The clapper boy did his bit.

'Scene thirty-four . . . take two.'

Desai waved the rifle and addressed Veera, 'Neela Devi, you do not have to Devi a thing. I have also had Peshawar's . . .'

'Cut, cut!' Ashok screamed like a banshee.

Desai placed the gun carefully on the floor and asked Ashok in a worried voice, 'Any mistake, Mr Ganguli?'

Ashok looked at Desai with murder in his eyes, then immediately assumed a lamb-like expression. 'None . . . it was very good . . . very, very good.' Then he said to me, 'Manto, come out for a minute.'

Ashok almost burst into tears as soon as we were off the set. 'Manto, what are we going to do? We have been at it since morning. He just doesn't seem to be able to say "the water of Peshawar" . . . Why don't we break for lunch?'

It was just as well because to expect Desai to get his lines right once his mind was derailed was one of nature's impossibilities. The trouble was that his retentive memory was absolutely zero. He just could not commit anything to memory, not even one line. If he was ever able to get his lines right, even one line, the first time, it was considered a pure accident. The funny thing was, no matter how many times he fumbled his lines, he remained totally unaware of his boo-boos. He had no idea which line he had turned into what. After rendering yet another rib-tickling version of the lines given to him, he would look at those present on the set, waiting to be complimented. One or two gaffes were always cause for general amusement, but when it went on and on, it was no exaggeration to say that everyone present on the set would have been more than happy to chop him up into a hundred pieces and be done with it.

I spent three years at Filmistan and during this period Desai made four films there. I do not remember a single occasion when he got his lines right the first time. He must have wasted hundreds of thousands of feet of film in his life. Ashok once told me that Desai's retake record stood at seventy-five. That was at Bombay Talkies. When he got it wrong for the seventy-fourth time, the German director Franz Osten wailed, 'Mr Desai, the problem is that the audience likes you. The moment you appear on the screen, it starts laughing. Had that not been the case, I would have lifted you myself and chucked you out today.'

During those seventy-four retakes, practically every studio employee had to be pressed into service to assure Desai that he was doing just fine. The trouble was that once he was in one of those grooves of his, nothing, including prayer, worked. The practice, therefore, was to go on shooting the same scene over and over again, hoping all the time that at some miraculous moment the will of God and Desai's memory would come together and the scene would get done as scripted.

During lunch break, as was the custom, nobody said a word to Desai about the botched lines for fear that it might remind him of the gibberish he had been speaking since morning. Ashok pretended to chat happily, while Desai kept up a steady humorous banter, which was not at all funny. However, everybody laughed at his jokes. When shooting was about to be resumed, Ashok asked, 'Desai sahib, do you remember your lines?'

'Yes, sir!' Desai answered confidently.

The lights came on. Scene thirty-four, take three began to roll. Desai waved his rifle in the air. 'Neela Devi . . . you . . . you.' He suddenly stopped. 'I am sorry.'

Ashok's heart sank, but to keep Desai in a good mood, he said, 'That's all right, but hurry up.'

Scene thirty-four, take four got under way. However, Desai was unable to separate urine from Peshawar. The trouble was that in Urdu the word for urine was 'peeshap', which was perilously close to Peshawar. When a few more efforts also failed to produce results, I took Ashok aside and said, 'Dadamoni, when Desai speaks his lines, let him say them with his back to the camera. Let him not drink the urine of Peshawar while facing the camera.'

Ashok immediately understood that this was the only way of getting out of this conundrum because we could then dub the lines in his voice by joining different sound clips. But, if he was facing the camera, his lip movements would not be in sync with the soundtrack.

When this was explained to Desai, he was shattered. He

assured us that this time he would get it right but the water was by now over our heads, and what was more, it was the water of Peshawar. We all begged him to go along and say whatever came to his lips. He was greatly disheartened. 'That is all right, Manto, I will turn my face away from the camera, but mark my words, I will get the lines letter perfect.'

'Scene thirty-four . . . take fourteen,' the words rang out. Desai waved his rifle in the air with a determined flourish and said to Veera, 'Neela Devi, you do not have a thing to worry about. I have also drunk the peeshap of Peshawar.'

'Cut!' Desai rested the rifle on his shoulder in triumph and asked Ashok, 'Yes, Mr Ganguly?' Ashok, whose heart by now had turned into stone, replied dryly, 'Fine, fine.' Then he said to Hardeep the cameraman, 'Let's do the next shoot tomorrow.'

We packed up the shift and I remembered that I had to go to Churchgate with a friend who was in a hurry to get to the railway station. As I stepped into the carriage, I found Desai sitting there bragging to his fellow passengers. I joined him. 'What should be done to those who forget their lines on the set?' I asked at one point.

Desai's answer was immediate. 'I don't know, I have never forgotten my lines, even once.'

He was innocence itself, being completely unaware of the disease called 'forgetting your lines'. I am quite sure he was convinced that he was incapable of making any mistakes. This was understandable because one can only be aware of mistakes if one knows what is right. Since that part of the human brain that makes such distinctions was altogether missing in Desai's case, he lived in a perpetual state of bliss. Those who thought him to be a great comedian were wrong. He was not even an actor. If people burst out laughing at what he did on the screen, the credit was due to nature's pulling mankind's leg. God had fashioned him out of funny bones.

Once at the racecourse, I pointed out Desai to my wife. She took one look at him from a distance and began to laugh. 'Why are you laughing when you can't even see him clearly?' I asked her.

She had no answer; all she could come up with was, 'I don't know.'

Desai was crazy about racing and would always bring his wife and daughter with him to the races, but he never bet more than ten rupees. He used to say that he knew many jockeys who gave him the inside dope which he passed on to his friends with instructions not to share the 'info' with anyone. Funnily enough, he never used those tips himself but relied on what someone else had told him. When I introduced him to my wife at the racecourse, he immediately gave her a 'sure' tip. When it failed to produce a winner, he told her in a surprised voice, 'How odd! This tip was supposed to be one hundred per cent accurate.' He himself had backed another horse, of course, which had placed.

Information about Desai's early life is sketchy. All I knew was that he came from a middle-class family of Gujarat. After his graduation, he took a law degree and for six or seven years knocked around Bombay's lower courts, making just enough to manage. Then he sort of flipped and remained half-crazy for some time. This was a very difficult time for him financially. His treatment had worked up to a point, but the doctors had warned him not to do any work involving intellectual activity or he might flip again. That was a tough one for Desai. Law was out because it required the brain to go full blast. He could have gone into business but he had no interest in it.

It was at this point that he asked Chiman Lal Desai of Sagar Movietone to get him some work at the studio. What he meant was a chance at acting. Since Chiman Lal was both a Gujarati and a Desai, he hired V.H. and because of him some directors gave him bit parts. However, all of them came to the conclusion that once was more than enough. For some time, V.H. remained at Sagar Movietone drawing a salary and doing nothing.

Meanwhile, Himanshu Rai had set up Bombay Talkies and had made a number of hit movies. This company was quite justifiably known for having a soft spot for educated people, so it was only a matter of time before Desai knocked at its doors. After two or three visits and a couple of letters of recommendation that he managed to obtain, he met Himanshu Rai. Because of his looks and despite his lunacy, Rai took him on, as he wanted to introduce an actor to the Indian cinema who was completely ignorant of the art of acting.

However, in his very first film, Desai became the centre of attention. What torture the staff and the technicians of Bombay Talkies suffered during the making of that movie, it is not possible to describe. Many times, they almost gave up on him but persisted because they saw it as a challenge. After his first film, Desai became a Bombay Talkies icon. No film coming out of that studio was considered complete or sufficiently amusing unless it starred Desai. He, of course, was delighted but not at all surprised because he was convinced that the secret of his success lay in his intelligence, application and tireless efforts; but as God is my witness, none of these things had anything to do with his fame and fortune. It was one of nature's jokes that Desai became Indian cinema's leading comedian.

During my time at Filmistan, he acted in three of its productions, *Chal Chal Re Naujawan*, *Shikari* and *Eight Days*. On numerous occasions, I nearly gave up on him, but since Ashok Kumar and Mukherjee had warned me what to expect, I persisted. It was a most trying experience. I have a restless temperament, so it is a wonder that I did not give up the ghost during the making of the first movie, *Chal Chal Re Naujawan*. There were days when I wanted to pick up the camera and throw it at him or push the sound boom down his throat and place all the studio lights on his immobile body. But one look at him and I could not help laughing.

I do not know how the angel of death was able to claim Desai's life. Didn't he roll over with laughter while approaching him? Even if angels do not have human characteristics, there can be no question that even for the angel of death it must have been a most amusing experience. I am reminded of the final scene in *Shikari* in which we had to kill Desai. It was the cruel Japanese who had to do the deed. However, he had a line to speak before dying. He was to tell his apprentice Badal, played by Ashok Kumar, and his beloved Veera that they should not grieve over his death but continue the good work. The nightmare of his lines was there, of course, as always; the problem was to have him die in a way that would not make the audience laugh. I had already announced my view that even if Desai was to be actually killed the audience would still laugh because they just would not believe that he had died or even that he could die.

Had it been left to me, I would have deleted this scene from the movie altogether, but the difficulty was that the direction the story had taken was such that Desai's character absolutely had to die. For days we toyed with various ideas but came to the conclusion that there could be no two ways about it: Desai simply had to die.

The lines did not really matter. We began to rehearse the scene. One thing that we all immediately noticed was that the way Desai died after having spoken for the last time to Ashok and Veera was extremely funny. This was supposed to be a poignant moment. The way he flailed his arms about made him look like a wound-up toy that was unwinding. This was bound to cause laughter. We told him to fall and not wave his arms about, but it seemed that, like his brain, his body too was not under his control. Finally, Ashok came up with a suggestion. He proposed that he and Veera, the heroine, should each grab Desai's hands so that he would not be able to wave his arms in that very funny way. Everyone was relieved that a solution had been found, but on the opening night, when this scene came, the entire auditorium burst out laughing. For the next showing, we partly edited the scene, but there was not much change in audience reaction. Finally, we decided to let it run as it had been shot.

Desai was a great miser and had never been known to spend a paisa on his friends. He had once bought Ashok's old car from him—on monthly instalments, of course—and since he could not drive himself, he employed a driver. However, we noticed that every ten days or so, he had a different one. When I asked him why, he gave me a roundabout answer. But soon the cat was out of the bag. Jagtap, the sound recordist, told me that every driver was hired without pay on a ten-day trial basis and was sacked on some excuse on the eleventh. This went on for several months, which gave Desai enough time to learn to drive himself.

Desai had long been an asthma patient and, on someone's advice, he had got into the habit of trying a little dried marijuana every day as an antidote. In winter, he would also help himself to a couple of glasses of brandy and then chirp merrily like a canary.

In *Eight Days* one of the scenes required him to sit in a bathtub. The weather was pleasant the day this scene was to be shot, but Desai kept complaining that it was cold. We had the water in the tub heated to keep him comfortable, while instructing the production manager to keep some brandy at hand. Those who have seen the movie will remember how Tekam Lala, which was his character's name in the film, gets into the bathtub in Sir Narindra's flat with an ice pack on his head and a fan blowing cool air in his face. He is supposed to have had a few drinks because he keeps saying, 'On all four sides is the sea and that big mountain made of ice . . .'

After the scene was shot and Desai had dried and changed, we gave him a large peg of brandy, which he downed happily. One peg was all it took to get him tipsy. He and I were alone in the room and he began to regale me with stories of his great exploits as a lawyer and how he used to score dramatic court victories for his clients. He was a great admirer of the legal acumen of Quaid-e-Azam Muhammad Ali Jinnah and Bhulabhai Desai. He had met the Quaid-e-Azam many times and heard him plead some of his celebrated cases.

While we were shooting *Eight Days*, I received a notice from Lahore, which said that the government of Punjab had issued warrants against me under Section 292 as my story 'The Odour' had been found to be pornographic. When I mentioned this to Desai, he began to brag about his encyclopaedic legal knowledge and this made me think of a prank. I decided that I would have Desai defend me. His mere entry into the courtroom would have people in stitches. When I mentioned this to Mukherjee, he agreed that it was a great idea. My list of defence witnesses also included the other great comedian of Indian cinema, Noor Mohammad Charlie. The mere thought of both these characters in one courtroom defending Saadat Hasan Manto was hilarious; Desai had begun 'preparing' my defence, which was totally unnecessary since all I wanted was entertainment. Noor Mohammad Charlie was also readying his testimony. Unfortunately, because of unremitting work at the studio, I found it impossible to get out of Bombay even for a day.

Desai was sorry that he had not found an opportunity to prove his legal genius. He did not, of course, realize that I had no interest in his knowledge of law. I had wanted him to do in court what he did in movies—to keep forgetting what he was supposed to say. I wanted him to make the court do one retake after another by turning Peshawar into peeshap and peeshap into Peshawar. Pity it never came to pass.

Desai has since died. The only time in his entire life when he did not need a retake or even a rehearsal was when he dutifully carried out the instructions of the angel of death and did exactly what he was asked to do, namely, slide into the valley of death without making any more people laugh.

RAFIQ GHAZNAVI: THE LADIES' MAN

I am not sure why, whenever I think of Rafiq Ghaznavi, I am reminded of Mahmud of Ghazni who invaded India seventeen times. If there was one thing common to the two of them, it was that they were both iconoclasts. While Mahmud ransacked the great temple at Somnath with its golden idol, depriving it of its treasures, Rafiq's conquests were made up of a dozen or so courtesans.

Rafiq's name would suggest that his ancestors came from Ghazni. I am not sure if he ever saw Ghazni; all I know is that he used to live in Peshawar and could speak both Pushto and Afghan Persian. Normally, he would speak Punjabi. He wrote well in English, and had he chosen to write in Urdu, he would have made a name for himself. He was much given to Urdu literature and his collection of books was large. When I first met him in Bombay at his Gulshan Mahal place and saw books scattered all over the floor, I was surprised. I had thought he was just a musician who had no use for literature, but when we began to talk he named authors of whom I had never heard. He told me about one Abdul Fazal Siddiqui who wrote stories only about animals and birds. When I read him later, I found him good.

I am not sure where I should start as I sit down to write on Rafiq Ghaznavi, but I have already begun writing and, if all goes well, I shall somehow reach the end. Let me try to remember when I first met him. I knew of him before we actually met. How I knew of him and for how long, I do not recall now. However, it must have been about twenty-five years ago when a betel-leaf seller in Bijli Chowk, Amritsar, called after me as I went past his shop. 'Babu sahib, it has been a long time. I think you should settle my account.'[1] I was taken aback because I had never taken any credit from him. 'What are you talking about? I have never bought anything here,' I said. He smiled. 'That's what they all say when they do not wish to pay what they owe.' I asked him for details and it was only then that I learnt that he had mistaken me for Rafiq Ghaznavi. I assured him that I was Saadat Hasan. 'But you bear a remarkable resemblance to him,' the shopkeeper remarked. I had heard of Rafiq Ghaznavi and until then I had had no desire to meet him, but when I heard that I looked like him I became curious.

Those days, I was wholly idle, restless and bored all the time. I wanted to sample everything I came upon, no matter how bitter the taste. I would go to shrines, walk in graveyards or spend hours sitting under a tree in Jallianwala Bagh, dreaming of the revolution that would destroy the British Raj in one instant. On seeing a bunch of schoolgirls on the street, I would pick one out and imagine that I was having an affair with her. I would try to invent bomb-making methods or would listen to noted classical singers and try to fathom the mysteries of their music. I once even tried my hand at poetry. I would write long love letters to sweethearts who did not exist, read them over and tear them up because they were such rubbish. I tried marijuana, cocaine and drinking but nothing cured me of my restlessness.

It was during that time that I developed an intense desire to meet Rafiq Ghaznavi. I looked for him at shrines, cheap drinking haunts and even asked about him in the bazaar where the dancing girls lived and performed, but no one could tell me where he was. Off and on, I would hear that he was in Amritsar and every time I heard that, I would go looking for him but never found him. One day, I learnt that he was in Amritsar and staying at the house of a friend, a tailor whose name I no longer remember. He had a shop in a small street of the Karmoon Deori area, not far from where I lived. When I went there, I was told that Rafiq was to be found at the tailor's home, which was outside the

---

[1]Manto wrote this piece around 1950–51, which would date his first meeting with Ghaznavi to 1925.

city in a thinly populated area. It was my friend Bala who had obtained the information for me. He was, in fact, on his way to this place and agreed to take me along. This is as good a place as any to introduce Bala. It pains me to write that he used to be known as Bala Kanjar—or Bala of the prostitutes' clan. I have never understood why human beings are associated with the professions of their families.

Bala was a young man of taste who was educated, handsome, witty and poetical. He had talent and much promise. He knew what people called him, but he did not care. He used to live in that area of the city where women make their living by selling their bodies. After Independence, he moved to Karachi and began to sell his paintings. I once read in a newspaper that he had held an exhibition of his works which had been greatly appreciated. Bala also liked to sing, though he had a bad voice. Along with him, Captain Waheed, Anwar the painter, Ashiq Ali the photographer, the poet Faqir Hussain Salees, and Giani Aror Singh the dentist formed our group of bohemians.

Most of our time was spent either at Anwar's or at the dental clinic of Giani Aror Singh. We could also be found at Jeeja's Hotel Shiraz or the shop of the tailor whose name I have forgotten.

While together, we would do marijuana. It would either be cooked with meat or ground into a mixture with milk and sugar. There would be much singing of the light classical variety— thumri, dadra and tappa. Ashiq Ali had a thin but sweet voice and he would often sing in Rafiq Ghaznavi's popular style. Captain Waheed played the tabla and Anwar just nodded his head and enjoyed the music. Giani Aror Singh would forget all about teeth and sing the raagni Pahari after the manner of Khan Sahib Ashiq Ali Khan of Patiala, son of Taan Kaptaan Khan Fateh Ali Khan. Ashiq Ali Khan's voice was awesome, deep and powerful in all three octaves. Bala used to tell jokes and, off and on, recite his latest poems. I still remember a verse, something about a teardrop dangling on an eyelash. It was good, as such poetry goes.

Giani Aror Singh was doing quite well as a dentist, but once the art bug bites you, you rarely survive, which was what happened. He closed down his business and disappeared. The same fate was in store for Anwar. I have no idea what happened to Jeeja, though I heard once that he was in Lahore practising herbal medicine. As for Faqir Hussain Salees, he went into soap-making. Giani Aror Singh eventually became a successful actor, but some time later I heard that he had renounced the world and become a hermit. Captain Waheed married a woman who already had five children. He became a contractor.

As for Rafiq Ghaznavi, he did not change. After moving to Pakistan, he raced horses in Karachi and composed music for the movies, which was exactly what he used to do in Bombay. I have begun to reminisce about things that happened a long time ago and I find myself getting carried away. I had begun writing about Rafiq and I went into unrelated things, though the truth is that it is these unrelated things which I like. Isn't life itself the sum total of unrelated happenings and people?

So here I was with Bala on my way to see Rafiq Ghaznavi. It was a cool evening in April and our tonga travelled for a long time before it came to a stop in front of a single-storey house in semi-darkness. Although this happened nearly twenty-five years ago, I distinctly remember that it was surrounded by trees and bushes. In the light of a lantern, that tailor whose name I cannot remember, and another character by the name of Meeda Mota, plus some others, were playing cards and drinking. I disliked Meeda Mota, first because he was fat, big and strong and, second, because he would always induce me to play cards, cheat and put me under a debt of eight or ten rupees. Some days later, he would waylay me, pull out a knife and ask me to pay, else . . . When Bala asked the tailor about Rafiq, he replied that he had been missing for two days, but he could not state with certainty where he was. Then he added, 'Bala, you know when Rafiq steps into a kotha he does not come out for weeks.' Bala smiled, which suggested that he knew that. As for me, another attempt to meet Rafiq had failed.

A year later, I saw a photograph of Rafiq Ghaznavi floating in a flat, open pan in Ashiq Ali's darkroom. Ashiq Ali was an innovative photographer, the first in Amritsar to use unorthodox techniques. Normally, photographers pander to the vanity of their subject by retouching all the lines in his face, lines that express his real character. They turn his face into a peeled potato without a mark or a line. Ashiq Ali used to say, 'It is the duty of the photographer to show people as they are. The camera must record what it sees accurately.' He loved using light and shadow, and the picture I saw that day was one of his masterpieces. Rafiq was dressed like an Arab. He had a long face and though some of it was in shadow I could see that his features, though not too sharp, were attractive. He was handsome. His nose was long and generously proportioned. His lips were thin and compressed, creating tiny triangles at either end, while his hair was long and swept back carefully, with long sideburns. I saw no resemblance between our two faces. God alone knows what that betel-leaf seller had seen in me that he thought I shared with Rafiq. Ashiq Ali told me that Rafiq had been at his studio a day earlier but had gone back to Lahore in the evening. So I went to Lahore after him, but was told that he had gone to Rawalpindi and since I had no intention of following him there I returned to Amritsar. A week later, I learnt that Rafiq had all along been cooped up in the kotha of a dancing girl. To hell with it, I thought. After this, years passed, but I still had not found an opportunity to meet Rafiq. In fact, I had nearly given up, though I kept up with the gossip, which had him sleeping with practically every leading courtesan of Amritsar.

Rafiq had popularized a certain style of ghazal singing and every girl in the bazaar dutifully followed it. The stories that went around about Rafiq had to be heard to be believed. 'And what is it that you are singing?' 'Oh, that is one of Rafiq's things.' 'And what style would that be?' 'Rafiq Ghaznavi's, of course.' 'You know, this smashed watch that you see is Rafiq's. Yesterday, as he began to develop a note, he waved his arm in the air and his hand hit the wall, smashing his watch into a thousand pieces.' 'Yesterday, Rafiq Ghaznavi was getting ready to sing at one of the kothas and had just finished tuning the instruments when he noticed something. "Tune your tabla," he said to the tabla player. "Done that already," the tabla player replied. "Do it one more time . . . there was a fly sitting on the right one a minute ago. It might have disturbed the tonal balance.'"

Rafiq also used to write poetry and one of his ghazals was very popular those days; I now confuse its words with one of Iqbal's, such being my memory. One day, I heard that Rafiq had gone to Lahore to play the lead in the first talkie being made in Punjab, based on the love legend of Heer Ranjha. Rafiq, being the hero, was Ranjha and the heroine was a courtesan from Amritsar by the name of Anwari (who later married Ahmed Salman of All India Radio—later of Radio Pakistan—whose Hindu name at birth was Jugul Kishore Mehra). The role of Qaido, the villainous uncle of Heer, had been given to M. Ismail. The film was made and released but I could not go to Lahore— why, I do not remember Rumours were rampant at the time that Rafiq had quarrelled with the movie's producer and director, A.R. Kardar, and also that Rafiq was having a torrid affair with Anwari, and that Anwari's mother was most upset and one of these days knives would be out and somebody would get hurt. Then came the news that Rafiq had run off with Anwari in a most dramatic manner.

The story was true. Rafiq really had decamped with Anwari, her distraught mother notwithstanding. Some really rough characters had been sent after Rafiq but they had failed to make him let Anwari go. Only when he was satiated did he send her back to her mother with the message, 'Here is your precious daughter—all yours.' This was a catastrophe for Anwari's family because a courtesan who is no longer a virgin fetches no price. The family had waited for the big day when the virgin Anwari would be 'married'—for a few nights—to the highest bidder, but now that she was 'soiled goods', it was not going to happen. The family, therefore, asked Rafiq to keep her. This was Rafiq's first recorded assault in this realm. Anwari eventually gave birth to a daughter, who was named Zarina—she played Roohi in A.R. Kardar's famous film *Shahjahan* (1946) and was later given in marriage by her 'father' Ahmed Salman, deputy director general of Radio Pakistan, to a rich businessman from Karachi.

In the meantime I left Amritsar and landed in Bombay where

I worked for various publications. There I learnt that Rafiq had left Anwari and was now in Calcutta writing film music scores. I too had moved to films, having wasted enough time in journalism. The first couple of years were spent chasing shadows but eventually I landed at Hindustan Cinetone owned by Seth Nanoobhai Desai, who had set up and bankrupted many film companies in his time. His new enterprise did not look too promising either. I had written the story for a movie called *Keechar*, which he had liked because it was based on socialist ideas. I never could understand why the seth, every inch a dirty capitalist, had taken a shine to it. One day, I was busy writing the dialogue for *Keechar* when someone said Rafiq Ghaznavi had just arrived and wanted to meet me. The first question that came to my mind was: How does he know me? I was still wondering when a tall, strapping fellow in a finely tailored suit walked into my room. It was Rafiq Ghaznavi. A fully articulated Punjabi curse rolled off his tongue, followed by, 'So you are hiding in here?' I suddenly had a feeling that I had always known him.

There was something carefree about Rafiq. The picture I had seen floating in Ashiq Ali darkroom in Amritsar was different from the real man in only one respect. It did not talk. His style of conversation did not go with his general personality. When he talked, his mouth opened in a cavernous way and I could not fail to notice that he did not have good teeth and gums. I would not have minded his bad teeth and gums if his conversation had not reeked of the bazaar. I did not like the way he moved his hands like a dancer when he talked. He spoke to me as he spoke to his social inferiors, which was something I disliked right away. However, since this was our first meeting and one I had sought for so long, I did not let these minor details affect my overall judgement of the man.

He invited me to come to his hotel in the evening. The first thing I saw when I entered his room was a vichitra veena, a stringed sitar-like instrument, which lay in a corner on the floor, sheathed in silk. In the other corner lay Rafiq's shoes in a neat row. Then I noticed a woman who appeared to have come straight from the bazaar—and, in fact, had. Her name was

Zohra. She later married a struggling film director by the name of Mirza and came to be known as Zohra Mirza. She had two children, a boy and a girl. The girl, who was older, was called Parveen and came to the movies under the name Shaheena. She made at least one film called *Beli* in the early days of Pakistan, based on one of my stories. It was a disaster at the box office. When I met Rafiq in Bombay, Parveen must have been around five. She had blue eyes, but Zohra, Parveen's mother, did not have light eyes. The girl had inherited her eyes from her grandmother who had lovely big blue eyes.

I forgot to record that when I was hired as a 'munshi' or resident writer at the Imperial Film Company, Zohra's two younger sisters had joined the outfit at the same time. One of them was rather plump, while the other was slim and pretty. Their names were Sheedan and Heeran. Sheedan was blithe, flirtatious and restless, and found it hard to sit still even for a minute. She spoke so rapidly that her words overrode each other. It was quite unnerving to talk to her. It was she who told me that Rafiq or Pheeko bhaijan, as she called him, had left Anwari and was now married to her (Sheedan's) elder sister Zohra. Heeran, compared to Sheedan, was awkward, which was why she could not make it in the movies, unlike her sister who had a part in Imperial's *Hind Mata*, which did quite well.

One day I went to Imperial Film Company to meet with Seth Ardeshir Irani, the owner. As I walked into his room through the swing door, I found him pumping one of Sheedan's breasts as if it was one of those old-fashioned car horns. I turned right around without saying a word.

To return to my visit, one look at Rafiq's room was enough to tell me that he was down on his luck those days. There was one thing about him. Whenever he was going through a bad patch—or what in Bombay is known as 'karki'—he would dress with the greatest care and in the most expensive clothes. Once he was over the hump, he would revert to ordinary clothes. He was one of those people who not only know how to dress but also look good in whatever they wear. We sat in his room for some time and then walked out into the hotel's small garden. I had brought a bottle of whisky with me, which we shared.

While there, we were joined by a woman. She smiled at Rafiq and took a chair next to him without any formality. Rafiq introduced her to me. She was a Sikh and had plenty of money of her own, but the film bug had bitten her and she had a crush on Ashok Kumar, which was why she came to Bombay every now and then, just to catch a glimpse of her idol. She was a big woman and Rafiq said to me in her presence, 'I have told this sali several times that she should cure herself of this Ashok Kumar obsession. Just think about it. Were Ashok to lie on top of her, he would look like a parrot trying to fire a cannon.' Rafiq kept laughing at his own joke for a long time. She did not react. That was another thing about him. He would laugh so much at his own stories that in the end those present had to join in. The Sikh woman had average looks and was slightly masculine in appearance. Although Rafiq kept conversing with her, it was clear that he had no interest in her. But that notwithstanding, he continued to drop broad hints about wanting to take her to bed. She, of course, had eyes only for Ashok Kumar. Finally, she told him in a characteristic rustic Punjabi way, 'Now listen, Rafiq, I would rather couple with a dog than . . .' But Rafiq did not let her finish. 'Say no more . . . you have no idea what a pedigreed dog I am!' Pedigree I do not know about, but what I would say is that Rafiq was indeed a dog though only courtesans and prostitutes could make him wag his tail. Housewives and straight women meant nothing to him.

This was our first real meeting and it led to many more. Rafiq was mean, selfish and low. He cared only about himself. He believed in accepting hospitality, but never offered any. However, if he had an axe to grind, he would throw a big party for you. But he would then scout the table and eat the best pieces of meat himself! He hardly ever offered anyone a cigarette. During the war it was difficult to buy good cigarettes except in the black market. One day, Rafiq walked into a studio where I was working, holding a tin of Craven A cigarettes, my favourite brand. When I tried to take one, he moved his hand so that the tin was beyond my reach. 'Let me have one,' I said. Rafiq stepped back, shoved the tin into his pocket and said, 'No, Manto . . . to begin with, I never offer anyone a cigarette; secondly, I do not want to spoil you. Go on smoking your Gold Flakes.' There were a couple of people around and I felt deeply humiliated.

Rafiq was utterly without a sense of honour although, as a Pathan, it was one quality he should have had. It was said that, before his affair with Zohra, he had had an affair with her mother. He had next seduced Mushtri, Zohra's elder sister, followed by Zohra and, finally, Sheedan, the youngest sister. Rafiq used to live on Bombay's Mahim Road. In fact, he lived in the same building as my sister. I was already married and living in Adelphi Chambers, Clare Road, where Rafiq used to visit me. We would also run into each other at All India Radio's Bombay station. One day I asked him, 'So what keeps you busy these days?' 'Love-making, but it is beginning to affect my health.' A few days later, I heard that Sheedan had tried to commit suicide by taking a large dose of opium. She must have pinched it from Zohra who, like her mother, had a taste for the drug. It turned out that there had been a fight between the two sisters over Rafiq. Zohra had told Sheedan that she was stealing her husband from her. Sheedan was too young and too infatuated with her Pheeko bhaijan to know what was good for her. Anyway, she survived and was spared the dubious honour of becoming a martyr to love. As a result of this incident, Rafiq left Zohra and set himself up with Sheedan.

When Rafiq's love life was at its most active, it so happened that a Hindu gentleman from Lahore came to Bombay with a young woman companion by the name of Zebunissa. He rented a flat in Gulshan Mahal on Lady Jamshedji Road in Mahim. He was a strange character. Obviously rich, he did not really care what his Zeb did as long as he did not know. He was quite happy with the way things were. Rafiq had somehow got to know him and had been over to his flat a couple of times, which was enough to have got Zeb interested in him. She was so taken with Rafiq that she would spend all her money on him and even bring him anything of value she found in her flat. The affair did not last as Rafiq got tired of her. When I asked why, he replied, 'She is too straight . . . not the sort of woman I enjoy.' He had no interest in women who were nice and homely, because the ones he had known all his life were from the bazaar, women who swore and drank and told dirty stories. He felt no sexual excitement if a woman showed 'wifely' qualities. He was husband to every prostitute and dancing girl who entered his semi-Byronic life. He was a very special client of these women, a client who gave nothing, but took what he could. He considered life itself to be some kind of a prostitute, a bazaar woman. He would sleep with it every night, get up in the morning and start exchanging dirty stories with it. Then he would ask it to perform, and return the favour by performing himself. He believed that was how life should be lived.

I never found Rafiq depressed. He was always shamelessly happy, which was perhaps the secret of his good health. His advancing years had done nothing to him; in fact, the older he grew, the more attractive he became to women. I used to say that when Rafiq reached the age of hundred, he would be transformed into a baby sucking its thumb.

When Sheedan give birth to a stillborn child, my wife and I went to his Shivaji Park place to condole. We saw a strange scene. Rafiq was sitting on the floor wearing a Turkish cap as if he were about to offer his prayers, while Zohra was dressed in black. She had not done her hair and her eyes were swollen. Mirza, the man she had married, was around and appeared to be rather overcome by the occasion. We heard Sheedan sobbing in the next room. Zohra leapt through the door and began to console her sister. It was all very odd.

Let me work it out. Rafiq was married to Zohra at one time and had two children by her, Parveen and Mahmood. He was now married to her sister Sheedan, and Zohra was married to Mirza. Sheedan was Zohra's sister as well as her sister-in-law. Rafiq's children by Zohra were Sheedan's nephew and niece and also her stepson and stepdaughter. Sheedan's stillborn child was Zohra's nephew as well as her stepson. Parveen and Mahmood were thus the stillborn baby's half-sister and half-brother, as well as his cousins. Rafiq and Mirza were brothers-in-law and so on and so forth. It was a mystifying rigmarole.

'Let's get out of here,' Rafiq said to me as we walked out on the veranda. He threw his cap on a chair and lit a cigarette. 'The hell with it . . . my face has become long because of the mournful expression I have had to wear since morning.' Then he burst out laughing.

Another time I had to travel to Lahore from Bombay to attend a court hearing. I met Rafiq there at an auction house run by one Syed Salamatullah Shah, a most colourful character. I was told that Rafiq was very happy as he had just returned from Amritsar where he had gone to meet his daughter by Anwari, Zarina alias Nasreen. Rafiq had only seen her as a little girl because Anwari had never encouraged him to visit her, having told her daughter that her father was an ugly rake. His friends arranged a meeting between Rafiq and the daughter he had only seen as a child. Rafiq told me that day in Lahore, 'Manto, she is tall and extremely beautiful, full of youth. When I took her in my arms and embraced her, it was like being in heaven.' I do not wish to comment on this statement. Rafiq also told me that when he was about to leave, Anwari came in and tried to pick a fight with him, but he silenced her with just one line. 'Shut up, Anwari . . . you should be grateful to me that I have made you the owner of a gold mine.' I have no idea how many such gold mines Rafiq gifted to how many women in his lifetime. I suppose we will only find out on the day of judgment. Rafiq once said to me, 'Frankly, I have no idea how many sons and daughters I have fathered. God alone knows because He is the greatest counter of them all.'

Rafiq also had a 'proper' wife, the one his family had found for him. She died three or four years after their marriage. They had a daughter by the name of Zahira, who was the film director Zia Sarhadi's first wife. The marriage ended in a divorce and the last I heard she was living in Karachi, where she had moved in 1947 with Rafiq Ghaznavi. That girl had a sad life but I hold Rafiq responsible for her ill fortune because he always advised her to live her life as he had lived his. When she was in Bombay, she got briefly involved with the film journalist Nazir Ludhianwi while she was also seeing Zia Sarhadi. Rafiq's advice to her was, 'Look child, if you cannot marry Nazir Ludhianwi, you should marry Zia Sarhadi, and if you can't make up your mind, you should marry both. If they betray you, don't take it to heart. Remember I am your biggest husband, being your father.' Nazir was betrayed by Zahira and Zahira by Zia. Subsequently, she came to live with the biggest husband of them all, Rafiq Ghaznavi. She used to smoke bidis, looking for her lost youth in their ashes, a youth which was destined to come to nothing. I do not wish to write another word about Zahira because I find it agonizing.

Rafiq was always very boyish. He would laugh at the slightest joke, and if he felt happy, he would actually jump up and down. At that time we were making *Chal Chal Re Naujawan* for Filmistan, starring Naseem and Ashok Kumar. Rafiq too was playing a role in it. He told me that he used to know Naseem's mother, the famous Delhi courtesan Shamshad alias Chammiya. One evening, with some of the city's richest patrons in attendance, she was singing and sipping a drink out of a crystal glass, when she noticed Rafiq, smiled and waved to him to come sit next to her. He said he sat there all night, taking one drink after another from her dainty hand. 'I was there for the next fifteen days and nights,' he told me. I introduced him to Naseem. The last time Rafiq had seen her, she was a little girl running around the room with a chunnariya over her head. Naseem knew Rafiq. Their conversation was rather stilted and formal because Naseem was always extremely polite. She did not allow Rafiq an opportunity to say anything 'loose', but he was thrilled to be in her company. When he came to my room, he began to dance and praise Naseem's beauty. He jumped on a table, dropped to the floor with a thud, swerved and swivelled for some time, then crept under a table, hit his head against it, re-emerged, stood up and started singing. I think Rafiq was quite keen to have something going with Naseem but he had no luck, not that he ever gave up trying.

Nur Jehan he would have seduced but she was so smitten by Shaukat Hussain Rizvi that she had no time for anyone else. Sitara, however, without quite wanting to and without being asked, ended up in Rafiq's bed, he having taken advantage of

her simultaneous affairs with Arora and Nazir. When Sohrab
Modi was filming *Sikander*, Meena, a young girl from Bombay's
courtesans' quarter, Pawan Pull, was also around, having been
spirited away by a man called Zahoor Ahmed, who had married
her. She had found a job in Minerva Movietone. Rafiq, who was
scoring the music for the movie, had written a chorus—*Zindagi
hai pyar se, pyar se bitai ja; Husn ke hazoor mein, apna sar
jhookai ja* (Life is love, spend it in the pursuit of love; when
you see beauty, bow down before it). Rafiq had duly bowed in
front of Meena but just three or four times. Then he rolled up
his prayer mat and disappeared.

Then there were those two singing girls from Agra, both
sisters, who had recently moved to Pawan Pull from Hyderabad,
where they had served the pleasure of Prince Moazzam Jah.
The elder one was called Akhtar, while the younger one, who
was only fourteen or fifteen, was named Anwar. They used to
perform at their kotha and were very popular. Haldia, a friend
of mine from Delhi, had a crush on Akhtar. On one of his visits
to Bombay, we spent an evening listening to the two sisters. I
don't know how but Rafiq Ghaznavi's name came up during our
conversation. 'He is a bastard,' I said. The younger one smiled
at me flirtatiously and said, 'You bear a close resemblance to
him.' I was left speechless.

I mentioned this exchange to Rafiq but he did not know the
girls. However, after some time he began to visit them. His
interest lasted just a year. His prediction that Anwar would
become a great thumri singer came true. I saw her several
years later at All India Radio's Delhi station where I was then
working. She was a bag of bones. The change was shocking.
Gone were her youth and vivaciousness. Who had reduced her
to this state, I wondered. She sat in front of the microphone, a
couple of pillows cradling her back, her head resting against the
tanpura to spare her fragile neck the burden of supporting that
weight. But when she sang, the listeners felt as if her voice was
penetrating their souls.

As for Rafiq, it was always my opinion that he was more of a
trick performer than a singer. He would have you swaying before

even a single note had left his lips. He would place his finger on one of the keys of his harmonium and his face would assume an other-worldly look. Then he would emit a long 'hai'—as if he was in pain or his soul was leaving his body—electrifying his listeners. This would be followed by another sound of unbearable pain (or was it pleasure?) and just when it felt that he was about to swoon, he would burst out laughing. The actual performance would come next, like water being sprinkled gently on parched earth. He would make strange faces when singing, as if his stomach was bothering him, especially when he was singing a classical composition. He appeared to be in such agony that you would pray to God to release him from his ordeal.

When Ezra Mir set up a film company in association with some other well-to-do Jews of Bombay and announced its first production, *Sitara*, Rafiq was chosen as music director. Mir was a handsome man and so were his associates, but even standing among them, Rafiq's personality was undiminished. He was the kind of man who stood out in a crowd. His style of work was unique. There he would be, standing in the middle of a hundred musicians and giving them their final instructions; with the Punjabis, he would crack jokes, while the Christian musicians would be addressed in English; to the Urdu-speaking ones, he would talk in chaste Urdu. One day Rafiq, Ezra Mir and I were together in Mir's room discussing a composition, while the musicians were in one of the studios rehearsing. Suddenly, Rafiq trained an ear in the direction of the music, which we could only hear faintly, pulled a face and said in an agonized voice, 'Dash it, one of the violins is not properly tuned.' Then he left us to attend to the offending instrument.

I have no taste for music and though I have listened to most of the great singers of our time, somehow I have never become privy to the mysteries of music. However, I do know that Rafiq did not have a good voice. I do not know enough about the subject to give an opinion about his knowledge of music. I have heard it said that when he sang, he was often off-key. I once told this to Nur Jehan. Her reaction was spontaneous. She put her tongue between her teeth and touched both her ears with

her thumb and index fingers. 'Oh no, oh no . . . this is calumny
. . . He was a master . . . one of a kind.' Age, she agreed, always
affected one's voice but there could be no question about Rafiq's
knowledge of music. It was his special gift.

But the special gift that Rafiq possessed in my view was his
utter lack of a sense of honour and shame. I would not call
him characterless because he was not an ordinary person but
an artist. He may not have believed in any religious edicts but
he always observed the basic ground rules. He may have been
nobody's friend but neither was he anyone's enemy. He was never
the traditional husband but, in all fairness, it must be pointed
out that he never expected any woman to play the traditional
wife to him.

There was this woman from one of Delhi's respected Hindu
families who fell in love with Rafiq. She would write him long,
rambling letters. I discovered this because I ran into Rafiq one
day and noticed that something appeared to be bothering him,
which was quite untypical. When I asked him what it was, he
told me the story. 'Manto, this girl has taken leave of her senses.
I am not a one-woman man. I do not believe in platonic love.
She says she is going to leave home and come to me . . . She can
if she wants to but how long will I be able to stay glued to her
pure love? I wish to God all good women would remain in their
homes, get married, give birth to children and go to hell. I am
all right without their pure, platonic love, thank you. All my
life I have dealt in counterfeit coins; it is too late for me to fool
around with real ones.' Then he wrote a coldly worded letter to
the girl from Delhi and never heard from her again.

This piece on Rafiq leaves me with a feeling of incompletion
because I cannot do justice to his multifaceted personality in a
handful of pages; but if I live longer, I promise to do a whole
book on him. Let me close with a story. When we were making
Chal Chal Re Naujawan, Rafiq invited all of us to dinner at his
flat in Shivaji Park: the producer S. Mukherjee, the director Gyan
Mukherjee, Ashok Kumar, Santoshi, Shahid Latif and myself.
Rafiq was sitting on the floor, humming, with a harmonium
in front of him. Next to him sat Sheedan and her brother. He

welcomed the others formally but greeted me with the usual jocular Punjabi abuse. We had a few drinks, but while the others were served Scotch, I was given Indian Solan whisky, which I drank quietly. In between, Rafiq would roll a swear word in my direction, but I was determined not to show any reaction. Finally, food was served and, as was to be expected, Rafiq served the best pieces of meat to himself. After eating, everyone left except me. Sheedan also retired but her brother kept me company. Rafiq, who was not much of a drinker, was dozing because of all the good food he had eaten.

My turn had now come. I rose, tiptoed into the next room, found the bottle of Scotch, which was still half full, brought it out and began to drink. Off and on, I would pour one for Sheedan's brother. Then I would try to wake up Rafiq but he would go back to sleep after swearing at me. It was my turn this time. So I began to curse Rafiq. I cursed him so much that he woke up, looking bewildered and overwhelmed. My vocabulary of swear words was limited, so I kept repeating the ones I knew, sometimes using them in new combinations. When this became too repetitive, I decided to say whatever came to my lips, nonsense words, swear words, all kinds of words.

Rafiq was drunk, sleepy and he felt helpless. In the end, he surrendered and begged me in a half-dead voice, 'Manto, please . . . I am exhausted, I have no strength left to return your abuse.' That was the moment I had waited for all evening. I felt that I was finally even with him. I am sure he will curse me when he reads this but since I am in Lahore and he is in Karachi, I am safe for the time being. When he comes to Lahore, I am sure I will get a mouthful from him. Then I will throw a party, pour spirit in a glass of Gymkhana whisky and drink it down.

SHYAM: KRISHNA'S FLUTE

It was 23 or 24 April. I do not really remember. I was in the mental hospital at Lahore, recuperating after having earlier gone on the wagon, when I read in a newspaper that Shyam was dead. I was in a strange state at the time, suspended between consciousness and a complete lack of it. It was not possible to determine where one ended and the other began. The two states had become intertwined in a way that was hard to work out. I felt as if I was in no-man's-land.

When my eye caught the news item about Shyam's death, I thought it had something to do with my having stopped drinking. In the past weeks, various members of my family had died in my semi-conscious condition; I learnt later that they were all well and alive and praying for my recovery.

I distinctly remember that when I read about Shyam, I said to the inmate in the room next to mine, 'Do you know that a very dear friend of mine has died?'

'Who?' he asked.

'Shyam,' I replied in a tearful voice.

'Here? In the lunatic asylum?'

I did not answer his question. Suddenly, one after another, several images sprang to life in my fevered brain: Shyam smiling, Shyam laughing, Shyam screaming, Shyam full of life, utterly unaware of death and its terrors. So I said to myself that whatever I had read in the newspaper was untrue . . . even the newspaper that I held in my hands was only a figment of my imagination.

But as time passed and the mist of alcohol began to lift from my mind, I reasserted my hold on reality. The entire process was so slow and drawn out that when I finally realized that Shyam was dead I did not experience any shock. I felt as if he had died long ago and I had mourned his passing at some remote point in

44

the past. Only the symptoms of that grief now lingered, a debris through which I was digging in the hope that in this broken mass of brick and stone I may somewhere find the buried smile that once belonged to Shyam, or the sprightly peal of his laughter.

Outside the mental hospital in the world of the sane, it was believed that Manto had gone mad after being told of Shyam's death. Had that actually happened, I would have been extremely sorry because Shyam's death should have made me wiser, heightened my awareness of the impermanence of the world. It should have made me acquire the vengeful determination to live to the hilt what was left of life. To have gone mad after learning of Shyam's death would have been madness itself.

Ghalib wrote that the legendary lover Farhad, when told of his beloved Shireen's death, killed himself with one blow of the instrument he was using to break stones. Ghalib did not consider this an act worthy of a great lover. Why had he terminated his life through a traditional, mechanical method? He should have just ceased to be. How could I, therefore, insult Shyam, who hated every conventional thing, by going mad?

Shyam is alive. He is alive in his two children, who are a result of his effulgent love for Taji whom he used to call 'my weakness'. He is alive in the person of all those women whose stoles of silk and muslin once brought shade and shelter to his loving heart. And he is alive in my heart which grieves because, when he was dying, I could not stand over him and shout, 'Shyam zindabad'.

I am sure he would have kissed death with the utmost sincerity and said in his characteristic style, 'Manto, by God, those lips are something else.'

When I think of Shyam, I am reminded of a character from a Russian novel. Shyam was a lover, but to him the act of love was not to be performed for its own sake. He was prepared to die for anything that was beautiful—and I think death must have been beautiful; otherwise he would not have died.

He loved intensity. People say the hands of death are cold, but I do not believe it. Had it been true, Shyam would have flung them aside and said, 'Go away woman, you have no warmth.'

He writes in a letter:

Pal, the long and short of it is that everyone here is 'hiptullha' but the real 'hiptullha' has gone far, far away. As for me, there appears to be no reason for complaining . . . Life is steaming ahead, good times and drinking, drinking and good times. Taji has returned after six months. She continues to be my one great weakness. And you know there is no greater pleasure in life than to experience the warmth of a woman's love . . . After all, I am a human being, a normal human being.

I run into Nigar [the actress Nigar Sultana] off and on, but the first right is that of 'T'. In the evenings, one misses your wise rubbish.

Shyam has used the word 'hiptullha'—and that needs an explanation.

I was working for Bombay Talkies. At the time, Kamal Amrohi's story *Haveli*, which was later filmed as *Mahal*, was being given the final touches. Ashok Kumar, Vacha, Hasrat Ludhianwi and I used to have discussion sessions every day where not only the story but all kinds of things, from gossip to scandal, came up. Shyam, who was shooting *Majboor* in those days, often joined us after knocking off work.

Kamal Amrohi was given to using heavyweight literary words and expressions even in normal conversation, which caused me problems because when I said something in simple words I could see that he was not impressed. And if I chose to say it in his heavy style, it would fly over the heads of Ashok and Vacha. Consequently, I had begun to employ a strange melange of words to make myself understood.

One morning while on the train from my home to Bombay Talkies, I opened the newspaper at the sports page to read the scorecard of a cricket match that had been played at the Brabourne Stadium, when I came across a strange name: 'Hiptullha'. I had never heard such a name before. I assumed, therefore, that it was a corrupt form of 'Haibatullah'.

When I got to the studio, the script conference was already in session. In his typical and ornate style, Kamal was describing one of the episodes. After he was done, Ashok looked at me. 'Well, Manto?'

I don't know why, but I heard myself saying, 'It is all right—but it lacks "hiptullha".'

Somehow 'hiptullha' managed to convey my meaning. What I wanted to say was that the sequence lacked force.

Later in the meeting, Hasrat presented the same sequence with variations. When I was asked my opinion, I said, this time consciously, 'Hasrat, dear friend, it doesn't do the trick. Come up with something which is hiptullha—I mean hiptullha.'

When I said 'hiptullha' for the second time, I looked around at the others for their reaction and was delighted to discover that the word had gained acceptance. In fact, it was used freely by everyone through the rest of the session, and with variations, such as: 'This thing has no "hiptullhity"' or 'It needs to be "hiptullhized".' At one point, Ashok collared me. 'What is the actual meaning of "hiptullha" and which language does it come from?'

Shyam had joined us by then. He began to laugh and his eyes narrowed. When I saw that odd name in the paper, he was with me on the train. Almost rolling over, he informed the meeting that it was Manto's latest Mantoism; when all else failed, he dragged 'hiptullha' into the film world. Soon the word gained popular currency in Bombay's film circles.

In a letter dated 29 July 1948, Shyam writes:

Dear Manto,
Once again you have gone silent and I am annoyed, really, although I am conscious of your mental lethargy. Anyway, I go berserk—and I cannot help it—when you suddenly slip into one of your silences. While it is true that I am no great letter monger myself, I get a special thrill out of receiving and writing letters, which are of a 'different kind', in other words, 'hiptullha'.

But 'hiptullha' has become a rare bird here. If you try to write it down on a piece of paper, it becomes 'hiptullhi' and if one can't even grab 'hiptullhi', you can imagine how annoying it can be. Excuse me if I have started 'hiptullhizing', but what can I do? When what is real gets lost, one begins to 'hiptullhate', but I don't give a damn as to what you think or what you don't. All I know is—and you can't be unaware of it—that I am the only person who has had the honour of humbling on the battlefield a big 'hiptullha' like you.

Manto, someone has said that when a lover runs out of words, he begins to kiss; and when a speaker runs out of words, he starts to cough. I want to make an addition to this saying: When a man runs out of manhood, he begins to look back on his past. But don't you worry, I am some distance yet from that final point. Life is full and it is rushing along. I find little time for that special madness, although I need it badly.

The film with Naseem [*Chandni Raat*] is nearly half-complete and I have signed a contract for one more with Amarnath. Guess who my heroine is. Nigar, and it was I who proposed her name, just to find out if it was possible to revive on the screen the feelings which we once felt for each other in real life. It was a joy once, but now it is work. But what do you think? Would this not be a lot of fun and frolic?

Taji is still in my life and Nigar is very good to me. She treats me with such gentleness. For some time now, Ramola has also been in Bombay and when I met her I discovered that she had not quite been able to overcome the weakness she once felt for me. So we have had some fun and games.

Old boy, these days I am receiving advanced training in the art of flirtation, but pal, this entire business is very complicated, and as you know, I love complications.

The wanderer, adventurer and seeker in me are still very powerful. I am not of a given place and do not wish to be of a given place. I love people and I hate people, so that is how life is passing. Come to think of it, life is my one and only sweetheart. As for people, they can go to hell.

I have forgotten the name of the author and all I

remember is this line—which may not even be correct—but what it says is, 'He loved people so much that he never felt lonely; and when he hated them he felt quite alone.' I cannot add to that.

In both letters, there is mention of Taji, which was what Mumtaz was called. And who was Mumtaz? In Shyam's own words, his 'great weakness'. The truth was that Nigar, Ramola and all of them were his weaknesses. Women were his greatest weakness, and also his greatest strength.

Mumtaz was the younger sister of Zeb Qureshi. She arrived in Bombay with Zeb and fell in love 'heavily', it should be said, with the thickset actor Zahoor Raja. However, she rid herself of him quickly and returned to Lahore where she met Shyam and thus their great romance began. When Shyam started to do well in Bombay, he married her for the sake of the children he wanted to have with her.

Shyam loved children, especially cute children, even if they were impertinent. In the eyes of the fussy and the snooty, Shyam himself was the most impertinent. Some women disliked him intensely because of his straight, no-nonsense style, but he didn't give a damn about that. He had never tried to 'improve' himself to win their approval. Shyam's exterior was a reflection of his inner self. 'Manto,' he would say, 'these salis who look down at me are fake—they live in an artificial world of cosmetics and make-up.'

There were some women, though, who loved him because he was rough and straight. They found his conversation utterly free of the lewd stench of the adulterous bed. Shyam would talk to them in an unselfconscious and open way and they would say things to him that would not be considered fit for utterance in polite society. Shyam would be there laughing his head off, jumping up and down, tears running down his face, and I would feel as if in a corner of the room, on a bed of sharp nails, lay the goddess called inhibition praying for forgiveness of his sins.

When and where I first met Shyam, I no longer remember clearly. It now seems as if I had known him even before we were introduced. Our first meetings, I am reasonably sure, took place on Lady Jamshedji Road where my sister had a place. On the top floor of a building called 'High Nest', lived a woman named Diamond. Shyam and I met on the stairs leading up to her flat a couple of times; these encounters were quite casual and informal. During one such encounter, Shyam told me that Diamond, who was officially known in the building as Mrs Shyam, was not his wife at all, though they were like husband and wife in all other ways. Shyam wasn't a believer in the fig leaf called marriage, though once when he had to get Diamond admitted to a hospital in order to deal with a certain 'problem', he had registered her in the records as his wife.

Long after the affair was over, Diamond's husband filed a suit against Shyam and the matter dragged on for quite some time. It was finally sorted out, because Diamond had by now entered the world of movies and seen the money-lined pockets of the men who inhabited it. Shyam was no longer a part of her life, though he would often talk about her.

Once I remember the two of us were walking in a park in Poona and Shyam said to me, 'Manto, Diamond was a great woman. By God, a woman who can bear the trauma of an abortion can face up to the greatest challenge in life.' Then he had paused. 'But Manto, why is a woman afraid to face the outcome of a relationship? Is it because she sees it as the fruit of her sin? But what is this rubbish about sin and virtue? A banknote can be genuine or fake; a child cannot be legitimate or illegitimate. It is not like putting an animal under the knife in the name of the God of the Muslims or decapitating it in the manner approved by the Sikhs. A child is the outcome of that divine and magnificent madness which first gripped Adam and Eve. Oh! That madness!' And then he had kept reminiscing about his innumerable bouts with that madness.

Shyam had a high-pitched personality. His conversations, his movements, his manners were all expressed in the higher notes. He was not a believer in the middle way. To him nothing could be more comical than to sit in company with a grave expression on your face. If, while drinking, someone fell silent or tried to philosophize, Shyam would blow his top. There were times when he would even smash the bottle and glasses on the table and storm out.

I remember an incident that happened in Poona. Shyam and the writer and poet Masood Pervez were both living in a house called 'Zubaida Cottage'. I was in town to sell a film story. Masood by nature was a quiet man and after a few drinks would go into a sepulchral silence. One day we began a rum drinking session quite early in the day. Many came, downed a few, got drunk and left. Only Masood, Shyam and I stayed the course. Shyam was in a great mood because he had been making much noise with the drunken ones practically all day. By evening he felt that Masood had isolated himself from us, perhaps having had too much of Shyam's raucousness. Shyam narrowed his intoxicated eyes, looked at Masood and said sarcastically, 'Hazrat Pervez, have you completed your elegy?'

Masood smiled in his characteristic manner and said nothing. Just at that point, in walked Krishan Chander, the short-story writer, and Shyam forgot about Masood Pervez and his frozen smile. After a couple of rounds, Shyam told Krishan about the 'unbearable iciness' of Masood. Krishan needed only two drinks to unlock his tongue, which happened quickly. 'What kind of a poet are you?' he said to Masood. 'You have been drinking since morning and you have yet to say something even slightly offensive. By God, a poet who cannot talk rubbish is incapable of writing poetry. I am astonished you actually write poetry. I am quite sure your poetry is rubbish. Look at yourself now. You've turned into a bottle of castor oil after all that good liquor.'

Shyam was so amused by this simile that he fell on the floor laughing, tears running down his cheeks.

We kept teasing Masood, but he did not react. Then suddenly he got up, emptied all our glasses in gulp after gulp and declared, 'Let's go.'

We stepped out of the house and, at Masood's suggestion, we took off our shoes, tucked them under our arms and began to run. It was around midnight and the streets of Poona were deserted. The four of us and another person, whose name

I cannot recall, were running like madmen and screaming our heads off, not knowing where we were headed and not particularly interested either.

At one point, we found ourselves in front of Krishan Chander's house and noticed that he had run ahead of us and gone in. We forced him to open the door and spent some time teasing him. His friend Samina Khatoon, who was asleep in the next room, woke up and came in to investigate. Krishan begged us to leave him alone, which we finally did. Then we hit the road again.

Poona is a city of temples and you have to walk barely a couple of hundred yards to come upon one. Masood's next act was to go into the first temple we passed, pull the cord and ring the bell. When we heard the sound, Shyam and I prostrated ourselves, our foreheads touching the bare road, piously intoning, 'Shiv Shambhu, Shiv Shambhu.' From then on, the bell of each temple we came across was dutifully sounded and after we had risen from our supplications, we would break into laughter. Once or twice we even woke up a priest, but before the astonished and bleary-eyed man could say anything, we were off.

At three in the morning, Masood Pervez stopped in the middle of the road and let out such a torrent of abuse that we could not believe our ears. In my entire life, I had never heard him utter one impolite word. I must also add that all the while that he was unburdening the choicest abuse I had ever heard, I felt that those words did not sit right on his tongue.

We returned to Zubaida Cottage at four in the morning and hit the sack, though Masood remained up, composing poetry.

Shyam was not particularly given to moderation when it came to drinking, but he remained in control. Like an experienced player, he would carefully survey the field around him and then try his best to stay within its confines. He used to say to me, 'I prefer fours—sixers I hit by pure chance.'

Here is a sixer.

A few months before Partition, Shyam moved over to my place from Shahid Latif's house. In Bombaiya, those were karki times. We were all extremely hard up, but there had been no let-up in our drinking which continued unabated. One evening, we all had had more than a few. Raja Mehdi Ali Khan, the poet and lyricist, was also around. A curfew used to go into effect every night. He was getting ready to go home when I told him, 'Are you out of your mind? You will be hauled up.'

'Why don't you sleep here? Taji is not around these days,' Shyam said jokingly.

Raja smiled. 'But I can never sleep on a spring bed, absolutely can't.'

Shyam fixed a huge measure of brandy in keeping with Raja's ample proportions and said, 'Drink this and you will sleep like a log.'

Raja downed the glass in one go. We kept talking about Taji for a long time. She had had a fight with Shyam and had gone to stay with her sister. They used to argue over trivial things every eight or ten days, but I had learnt not to interfere because Shyam did not like it. There was an unstated understanding between us that we would not interfere in each other's private affairs.

Taji had gone with such finality this time that it seemed she would never come back. Shyam had said goodbye to her in a manner that suggested that he did not expect to see her again and wouldn't want to, anyway. However, they both pined for each other. In the evenings, Shyam would get so sentimental over Taji that I would be sure he would stay awake the rest of the night thinking of her. But he was so fond of sleeping that he would be gone minutes after hitting the bed. There were only two rooms in my flat; one was used as the bedroom, the other as a lounge. I had given the bedroom to Shyam and Taji, and I would sleep in the living room on a mattress placed on the floor. Since Taji was not around, Raja Mehdi Ali Khan was allotted one of the two beds in that room. It was very late when we turned in.

I woke up, as was my habit, at a quarter to six in the morning and noticed that somebody was lying next to me. It couldn't be my wife because she was in Lahore. When I rubbed my eyes and could see clearly, I found it was Shyam. How had he got here? Then I smelt burnt cloth. There was a sofa next to the mattress which had a hole burnt in it because of a cigarette that had not been put out properly. But that had happened many months ago.

How could it be smouldering after all this time? I was now more or less awake and could feel the sting of smoke in my eyes. I could also see a faint cloud of smoke in the air. I walked into the bedroom and found that the bed on which Shyam used to sleep was smouldering, while Raja was sound asleep on the other, his big mound of a belly undulating with the rhythm of his snores.

I examined the burnt mattress carefully and found that it had a hole as big as a dinner plate, which was emitting whiffs of smoke. It appeared as if somebody had tried to put out the fire because there was a lot of water on the bed, but since the mattress was lined with coconut fibre and cotton, the fire had not been killed fully. I tried to wake up Raja but he turned on his side and began to snore even more loudly. Suddenly, a red flame leapt out of the black hole in the mattress. I ran into the bathroom, filled a bucket with water and extinguished the fire completely. Then I woke up Raja, which was not easy because he had little intention of getting up.

When I asked him what had happened, he replied in his typical style, exaggerating the events of the night and inventing all kinds of details, swearing they were all true. 'This Shyam of yours is actually Maharaj Hanuman, the monkey god. Last night, after immersing myself in a pool of brandy, I went to sleep. At about two in the morning, I heard strange sounds, which woke me up. I saw Shyam who had turned into Hanuman, with his tail on fire. He was jumping up and down on the bed, trying to set it on fire with his tail. When it caught fire, I closed my eyes and dived into the pool of brandy and hit the bottom. I was about to stay there for the rest of the night when it occurred to me that if I did that your poor bed would turn into ashes. I got up and found Shyam missing. I went to the next room to awaken you and apprise you of the situation, but found Shyam, who had once again resumed his human form, sleeping next to you. I tried to wake you up. I screamed out your name. I sounded gongs, even detonated a couple of atom bombs, but you just would not get up. Finally, I whispered in your ear, "Get up, Khwaja, a whole crate of Scotch whisky has just arrived." You immediately opened your eyes and asked, "Where?" I said, "Wake up . . .

the house is on fire . . . fire, you understand? Fire." "Don't talk rubbish," was your answer to that. In the end, you decided to believe my statement, but returned to sleep after advising me to inform the fire brigade. Disappointed by you, I tried to awaken Shyam and explain to him the delicacy of our situation. When he finally managed to follow what I was saying, he said, "Why don't you put it out, pal? It is after all every citizen's duty to do so." Then, gathering all my feelings for humanity in my hands, I became a virtual fire brigade. Picking up the jug I had once given you for your birthday and filling it with water, I poured the contents down that hole in the mattress and since my job was done, leaving the rest to God, I went to sleep.'

When Shyam woke up after having slept his full quota, Raja and I asked him how the fire had started. He did not seem to know what we were talking about. After thinking long and hard, he said with finality, 'I am unable to shed any light on the incident involving a fire.' We went to the next room, picked up Shyam's badly singed silk shirt and brought it to him. He took one look at it and declared, 'An investigation is called for.'

Our joint inquiry revealed that the vest Shyam was wearing had two or three burn marks. And two burn marks on his chest, big and round like rupee coins, provided further evidence that he had had a brush with last night's fire. It was at this point that Sherlock Holmes said to his friend Dr Watson, 'It now stands conclusively proved that there definitely was a fire and Shyam left the bed quietly to go to the other room to spare his friend Raja Mehdi Ali Khan any discomfort.'

When Shyam married Taji in a regular ceremony to satisfy social conventions, it was my view that the huge party he threw was just his way of getting even with those who had drawn up such customs. This party remained the talk of the film world in Bombay for a long time. Enormous quantities of liquor were downed that night but the ugly spots on the scanty cloth with which polite society always insists on covering itself refused to come off.

Shyam was not only a lover of women and drinking, he loved every good thing in life. He loved a good book as much as he loved a good woman. He had lost his mother as a child but he loved his stepmother just as if she were his real mother. He loved his stepbrothers and sisters more than he would have loved his own siblings. After his father's death, it was he who looked after the entire family, which was quite large.

For a long time and with the utmost devotion, he tried to get rich and famous, but lady luck would always give him the slip at the last moment. Shyam never let these setbacks get him down. He would say, 'Sweetheart, one day you are going to land in my arms.' And sure enough, the day did come when he became both rich and famous. When he died, he was earning thousands of rupees a month and he lived in a lovely house in the Bombay suburbs. There had once been days when he didn't have a place to stay, but even during those times of dire poverty, he was the same happy and perennially smiling Shyam. When the two ladies called Fame and Fortune came, he greeted them not as people greet deputy collectors; he made them sit next to him on his wrought-iron bed and planted big kisses on them.

During those days of hardship Shyam and I shared a place. Our economic condition was quite unspeakable. Like the politics of the country, it was passing through a most delicate phase. I was employed at Bombay Talkies, and Shyam had just signed a contract with the studio for a movie and had been given ten thousand rupees. This bonanza had come his way after months of unemployment. However, though contracts were signed, money was never paid on time. But we always used to manage somehow. Had we been husband and wife, there would have been arguments over money, but as far as Shyam and I were concerned, we never kept an account of who was spending what.

One day after a great deal of haggling, he managed to get five hundred rupees from the studio, quite a large sum of money at the time. I was absolutely broke. We were both on the train returning home from Malad. On the way, Shyam decided that he had to see a friend in Churchgate. My stop came first, but before I got down, he shut his eyes, took out a thick wad of banknotes from his pocket, divided it down the middle without counting and said, 'Hurry up, Manto . . . pick any.'

I took one, slipped it into my pocket and got down. As the train moved, Shyam said, 'Ta ta,' pulled out another wad of money and waved it in the air. 'What do you think? For the sake of safety, I had kept some of the loot aside . . . Hiptullha!'

In the evening, when Shyam returned, he was not in a good mood. The friend he had gone to see was KK (which was how the actress Kuldip Kaur was known among friends), who had wanted to speak to him in private. Shyam poured a large measure from the bottle of brandy tucked under his arm and told me, 'The private matter that she wanted to talk about was that once, in Lahore, I had told someone that KK had a massive crush on me. But in those days I had no time for her. Today, she said to me—and I was at her house—that what I had said in Lahore was rubbish and she had never had a crush on me. So I said to her. "Well, you can develop one tonight." She tried to play it haughty and I hit her with my fist.'

'You hit a woman?' I asked.

Shyam showed me his hand, which was injured. 'The witch moved aside and I ended up hitting the wall.'

Then he laughed for a long time. 'Sali! She is just playing hard to get.'

I have mentioned money earlier . . . Two years ago, I was in great mental agony because of the state of Lahore's film industry and the obscenity case filed against me because of my story 'Thanda Gosht'. I had been convicted by the lower court and sentenced to three months in jail with hard labour and fined three hundred rupees. I was so disillusioned that I wanted to throw everything I had ever written into the fire and start doing something else which had nothing to do with literature. Perhaps a job at an octroi post with plenty of bribe money so that I could take proper care of my family. I no longer wanted to criticize anyone or even offer an opinion on anything.

It was a strange time of frustration and listlessness. Some people were of the view that my actual profession consisted of writing stories and then having them tried in court on an obscenity charge. Some said I wrote because I sought cheap fame, while others were of the opinion that I derived satisfaction from exciting people's baser sentiments. I had been tried four times and I alone knew what those four cases had done to me.

Not that I had been doing all that well anyway, but the last thing I now wanted to do was write. I would spend most of my time away from home, hanging around with people who had nothing to do with literature. In their company, I was busy committing physical and spiritual suicide.

Then one day I received a letter from the proprietor of Tehsin Pictures, the film distributors. He wanted me to see him without delay because he had received some instructions from Bombay. Just to find out who the sender of those instructions was, I went to their office and was told that Shyam had sent telegram after telegram from Bombay, urging them to find me wherever I was and give me five hundred rupees. When I arrived at Tehsin Pictures, someone was writing a reply to yet another telegram from Shyam, saying that despite efforts they had been unable to find Manto.

I took the five hundred rupees and tears welled up in my intoxicated eyes. I tried very hard to write a note of thanks to Shyam and to ask him why he had sent me this money. Did he know how hard up I was? I wrote many letters but tore them all up because they read like a mockery of the feelings that had prompted Shyam to send me the money.

A year ago when Shyam came to Amritsar for the release of one of his films, he also came to Lahore and asked many people about me as soon as he arrived. I had already come to know that he was in Lahore, and I practically ran out of the house to be at the cinema where he was going to appear after a dinner.

With me was Rashid Attrey, the music director and Shyam's old friend from Poona. When Shyam drove up in front of the cinema and saw us, he screamed and told the driver to stop the car. However, so thick was the crowd of fans that the driver could not do so. With him was the actor Om Prakash. Both of them were wearing similar clothes and Panama hats. They entered the cinema from the back door, while we went in from the front. It was the same Shyam, laughing, smiling, full of life.

He ran forward and threw his arms around us and we made

so much noise that nobody could follow a word. We were talking about a hundred things, all at the same time, and we buried ourselves under a heap of conversation. Once the public ceremony at the cinema was over, he took us with him to a film distributor's office. It was impossible to have a coherent conversation because we were constantly being interrupted and the flood of people was unremitting. In the street outside, a crowd had gathered because word had spread that Shyam was in there. The crowd was demanding that he should come to the balcony so that they could see him.

Shyam was in a strange mental state. He was intensely conscious of his presence in Lahore, the same Lahore whose streets had once been witness to his numerous romances. This Lahore was now thousands of miles from Amritsar. And how far was his beloved Rawalpindi where he had spent his boyhood? Lahore, Amritsar and Rawalpindi were all where they used to be, but those days were no longer there, nor those nights which Shyam had left behind. The undertaker of politics had buried them deep, only he knew where.

Shyam said to me, 'Stay by my side.' But his emotional agitation had reduced me also to such a state that I did not want to stay. Promising to meet him at Faletti's Hotel in the evening, I came home.

I had met Shyam after such a long time, but instead of happiness I felt an inexpressible melancholy. I was so upset that I wanted to get into a physical fight with someone, beat him up, get beaten and when exhausted, fall asleep. I tried to analyse my feelings but it was like untangling badly messed-up thread. I felt even more miserable when I went to Faletti's where I began to drink in a friend's room.

At about nine or nine thirty, there was a noise outside and I knew that Shyam had returned. His room was full of people who wanted to meet him. I sat there for some time but I could not talk to him. It seemed as if someone had put a lock on our feelings and threaded the keys in a huge ring with other keys, which the two of us were now trying to find.

I felt tired. After dinner, Shyam made a very emotional speech but I did not listen to a single word. My mind was broadcasting on a different and louder frequency. When Shyam finished his rubbish, the crowd roared its approval and broke into applause. I left and went to his room where film director Fazal Karim Fazli was already waiting. We had an argument over something very trivial. When Shyam arrived, he said, 'All these people are going to Hira Mandi, come with us.'

I almost began to cry. 'I don't want to go, you go and let your people go.'

'Then wait for me . . . I won't be long.'

Shyam left with the group that was going to Hira Mandi. I sat there, abused Shyam and the entire film industry, and said to Fazli, 'I think you will wait here, but if it is possible, please drop me home in your car.'

I had strange disjointed dreams all night. I fought with Shyam several times. In the morning when the milkman came, I was saying in hollow anger, 'You scoundrel, you are mean, you are disgraceful . . . you are a Hindu.'

I woke up and felt as if the greatest word of abuse in the world had just left my lips. But when I looked inside my heart, I knew that it was not my mouth but the blower of politics which had disgorged that vile word. While I took milk from the vendor which was one-fourth water, I thought of Shyam. I felt great solace at the realization that though Shyam was a Hindu, he was not a mixed-with-water Hindu.

Once, during the time of Partition when a bloody fratricidal civil war was being fought between Hindus and Muslims with thousands being massacred every day, Shyam and I were listening to a family of Sikh refugees from Rawalpindi. They were telling us horrifying stories of how their people had been killed. I could sense that Shyam was deeply moved and I could understand the emotional upheaval he was undergoing. When we left, I said to him, 'I am a Muslim, don't you feel like murdering me?'

'Not now,' he answered gravely, 'but when I was listening to the atrocities the Muslims had committed . . . I could have murdered you.'

I was deeply shocked by Shyam's words. Perhaps I could have also murdered him at the time. But later when I thought about it—and between then and now there is a world of difference—I suddenly understood the basis of those riots in which thousands of innocent Hindus and Muslims were killed every day.

'Not now . . . but at that time, yes.' If you ponder these words, you will find an answer to the painful reality of Partition, an answer that lies in human nature itself.

In Bombay, the communal atmosphere was becoming more vicious by the day. When Ashok and Vacha took control of the administration of Bombay Talkies, all senior posts somehow went to Muslims, which created a great deal of resentment among the Hindu staff. Vacha began to receive anonymous letters that threatened him with everything from murder to the destruction of the studio. Neither Ashok nor Vacha could care less about this sort of thing. It was only I, partly because of my sensitive nature and partly because I was a Muslim, who expressed a sense of unease to both of them on several occasions. I advised them to do away with my services because the Hindus thought that it was I who was responsible for so many Muslims getting into Bombay Talkies. They told me that I was out of my mind.

Out of mind I certainly was. My wife and children were in Pakistan. When that land was a part of India, I could recognize it. I was also aware of the occasional Hindu–Muslim riot, but now it was different. That piece of land had a new name and I did not know what that new name had done to it. Though I tried, I could not even begin to get a feel for the government which was now said to be ours.

The day of Independence, 14 August, was celebrated in Bombay with tremendous fanfare. Pakistan and India had been declared two separate countries. There was great public rejoicing, but murder and arson continued unabated. Along with cries of 'India zindabad', one also heard 'Pakistan zindabad'. The green Islamic flag fluttered next to the tricolour of the Indian National Congress. The streets and bazaars reverberated with slogans as people shouted the names of Pandit Jawaharlal Nehru and Quaid-e-Azam Muhammad Ali Jinnah.

I found it impossible to decide which of the two countries was now my homeland—India or Pakistan. Who was responsible for the blood that was being shed mercilessly every day? Where were they going to inter the bones that had been stripped of the flesh of religion by vultures and birds of prey? Now that we were free, had subjection ceased to exist? Who would be our slaves? When we were colonial subjects, we could dream of freedom, but now that we were free, what would our dreams be? Were we even free? Thousands of Hindus and Muslims were dying all around us. Why were they dying?

All these questions had different answers: the Indian answer, the Pakistani answer, the British answer. Every question had an answer, but when you tried to look for the truth, none of those answers was of any help. Some said if you were looking for the truth, you would have to go back to the ruins of the 1857 Mutiny. Others said no, it all lay in the history of the East India Company. Some went back even further and advised you to analyse the Mughal empire. Everybody wanted to drag you back into the past, while murderers and terrorists marched on unchallenged, writing in the process a story of blood and fire, which was without parallel in history.

I stopped going to Bombay Talkies. Whenever Ashok and Vacha dropped in, I would pretend I wasn't feeling well. Shyam would look at me and smile. He knew what I was going through. I began to drink heavily, but got bored and gave it up. All day long, I would lie on my sofa in a sort of daze. One day, Shyam came to the flat straight from the studio. I was lying listlessly on the sofa. 'Chewing the cud, Khwaja, are we?' he asked.

I was upset. Why did he not think like me? Why did he look so calm? Why did he not feel the terrible upheaval that was raging through my heart and soul? How could he keep laughing and cracking jokes? Or had he perhaps come to the conclusion that the world around us had gone so completely insane that it was futile even to try to make sense of it?

It happened suddenly. One day I said to myself, 'The hell with it all. I am leaving.' Shyam was shooting that night. I stayed up and packed. He came quite early in the morning, looked around and asked, 'Going?' 'Yes,' I replied.

We never mentioned the subject again. He helped me move odds and ends around while keeping up a steady patter of amusing stories about the night's shooting. He laughed a lot. When it was time for me to leave, he produced a bottle of brandy, poured out two large measures, handed me a glass and said, 'Hiptullha!'

'Hiptullha!' I answered.

Then he threw his arms around me and said, 'Swine!'

I tried to control my tears. 'Pakistani swine,' I said.

'Zindabad Pakistan,' he shouted sincerely.

'Zindabad Bharat,' I replied.

Then we walked down the stairs to a truck waiting to take me to my ship that was bound for Karachi.

Shyam came to the port. There was still time to board the ship. He kept telling funny stories. When the gong was sounded, he shouted, 'Hiptullha!' one last time and walked down the gangway, taking long, resolute strides. Never even once did he look back.

From Lahore, I wrote him a letter, to which he answered on 19 January 1948.

Everyone misses you and feels the absence of your upbeat humour, which you used to squander on these characters with such generosity. Vacha says you left without telling him; he finds your leaving paradoxical, since you were the one man who used to oppose the entry of Muslims in Bombay Talkies and it was you who became the first to run off to Pakistan, thus becoming a martyr to your own credo . . . However, that is Vacha's view and I hope you have written to him, and if you haven't, decency demands that you do.

Yours,
Shyam

It is 14 August today, the day when India and Pakistan became free. There are celebrations on both sides, and at the same time, full preparations for attack and defence are in hand . . . I say to Shyam's spirit, 'Dear Shyam, I left Bombay Talkies. Can't Pandit Nehru leave Kashmir? Now isn't that hiptullha?'

KULDIP KAUR: TOO HOT TO HANDLE

KK they called her, short for Kuldip Kaur. She appeared in countless films. Whenever I saw her name flashed across a billboard, I would always think of her nose because she had the pertest nose I have ever seen on anyone.

When Punjab was engulfed in communal rioting at the time of Partition, Kuldip Kaur was in Lahore making movies. She left for Bombay with the actor Pran, who was like her male mistress. He had already made a name for himself through his roles in films produced by Pancholi Studio. He was a handsome man and a popular figure in Lahore because of his impeccable clothes and the most elegant tonga in the city, which the rich of those days used for joyrides in the evening. I am not sure when the affair between Pran and Kuldip began because I was not living in Lahore at the time, but such liaisons between people in the movie world are not uncommon. During the making of a film, an actress could be carrying on with more than one man associated with the production. While the affair between Pran and Kuldip was on full blast, Shyam returned to Lahore, a city he loved to distraction, after having tried his luck in Bombay. A ladies' man by nature, it was only a matter of time before he turned his attention towards Kuldip. They would certainly have had a fling had another woman, Mumtaz, later popularly known as Taji, not entered Shyam's life just at that point.

Kuldip was offended by Shyam's sudden change of course and never forgave him. She was not the kind of woman who changes her mind once it is made up. One day in Bombay, the three of us—Shyam, Kuldip and I—were going home by train and it so happened that we were the only occupants of our first-class carriage. Shyam was boisterous by nature and, when he realized that he was practically alone with Kuldip, he began to flirt with her, hoping, of course, to pick up the thread from where he had let it drop in Lahore. He had just had a fight with Taji. Of his other friends, the actress Ramola was in Calcutta, and Nigar Sultana was currently the mistress of the lyricist Dina Nath Madhuk. So, in his own words, he was 'empty-handed'. He was teasing Kuldip. 'Sweetheart, why are you always trying to slip away from me? Why don't you sit next to me?' Kuldip's nose looked even more pert as she replied sharply, 'Shyam sahib, don't try these tricks on me.' I recall the rest of the conversation, but on second thought, I would rather leave it out because it was quite risqué. Shyam was incapable of speaking in a serious manner so, in his characteristic style, he said to Kuldip, 'Darling, dump that owl's offspring you call Pran and come to me. He is a friend of mine; I will explain it to him.'

Kuldip, with her pert nose and big eyes which she used to full effect, replied even more sharply, 'Keep your paws off me.' This kind of rebuff from women never had an effect on Shyam. He laughed. 'Sweetheart, you used to be mad about me in Lahore, or have you forgotten?' Kuldip now laughed sardonically. 'You fool yourself.' 'That is not true. You were mad about me,' Shyam insisted. I looked at Kuldip and I could feel that she still had a crush on Shyam but her obstinate temperament was in the way, so she batted her eyes a few more times and replied, 'I was, but no longer.' Shyam's response was typical of him. 'Look, if not today, then tomorrow, you are fated to come to me.' Kuldip was angry. 'Look here Shyam, let me tell you for the last time that there can never be anything between us. You just stop preening yourself the way you do. It is possible that I might have fancied you once in Lahore, but since you showed indifference then, I am determined to have nothing to do with you now. You'd better forget that Lahore business here and now.' There the matter ended, but only for the time being as Shyam did not have the patience for long discussions.

Kuldip came from a rich Sikh family of Attari in Punjab, one of whose members had a long relationship with a Muslim woman from Lahore. It was said to have continued after Partition. He was also believed to have spent millions on her. After 1947, he continued to come to Lahore, stay at Faletti's Hotel, spend a few days with his friend and return home.

During the division of the country, Pran and Kuldip had left Lahore in such a hurry that Pran's car—which Kuldip had probably paid for—had to be abandoned. Kuldip, not one to be afraid of anything, including men, whom she could wrap around her little finger, came to Lahore while the communal rioting was in full fury and drove the car all the way back to Bombay. I only came to know the story when I once asked Pran about his car. Kuldip had driven back without incident, he told me, except for a 'minor problem' in Delhi, but he did not say what it was. She told me once about the atrocities the Muslims had committed against Sikhs. The way she narrated those stories almost convinced me that she was about to pick up a butter knife from the table and plunge it in my belly. But she was just being emotional. She was not the kind of person who would have borne the Muslims any grudge for being Muslims. She was not religious in that sense but a woman who believed in pure animal instincts.

Kuldip's nose made her face look highly expressive. She had finely chiselled features and she talked with great intensity. When I left Filmistan and joined my friends Ashok Kumar and Savak Vacha at Bombay Talkies, it was clear to everyone that we were living in unsettled times and there was not much work to be had. One day Kuldip and Pran came to Bombay Talkies to see if there was something going. I had met Pran earlier through Shyam and we had become friends immediately, as he was a man without malice towards anyone. My relationship with Kuldip was on the formal side. But it so happened that three films were about to go into production at Bombay Talkies and Vacha, after taking one look at Kuldip, asked our German cameraman Josef Wirsching to do a screen test on her. Wirsching had come to Bombay from Germany with Himanshu Rai and had been placed under detention at Devlali during the war. He was released only after the war and he returned to Bombay Talkies. He was a good friend of Vacha's, head of the sound recording laboratory at the studio.

The lights came on while Kuldip Kaur went to the make-up room. Wirsching stood waiting behind a new camera, his cigar in his mouth. Kuldip appeared after some time and stood facing the camera without any self-consciousness. She was ready for action but I noticed that the German felt somewhat overawed by her presence. When he saw her through the lens, he was bewildered because from whichever angle he framed her, all he could see was her pert nose. He began to sweat, then turned to me. 'Let's have a cup of tea in the canteen.' I could guess what his problem was. As we sat down with our cups, he wiped his brow and said, 'Mr Manto, what can I do with her nose? It practically plunges into the lens. Her face merely follows.' Then he brought his lips close to my ear and whispered, 'And she is not quite right there, but how can I tell her?' He was referring to the fact that she was less than well endowed. Nose, he said, he could somehow manage but 'the other thing', well, some way would have to be found to deal with it. I assured him that I would get 'the other thing' worked out, and I did. When Kuldip was leaving the studio, I told her in plain words what Wirsching had said. I also told her that for thirty-five rupees, she could purchase at the Whiteway Laidlaw store something that would do the trick. The test in the meanwhile had been put off for a day.

Kuldip was not in the least bashful. She said it was no big deal and she would do the necessary, which she did right away. The next day when she came to the studio, she was a different woman. I silently saluted the inventors of these most ingenious devices. Wirsching took one look at her and was satisfied. He was still bothered about her nose, but 'the other thing' being the way he wanted it, he took her screen test and when we saw it in the projection room later everyone agreed that she was fine, especially in roles depicting 'the other woman'.

Off and on, Kuldip would come with Pran to one of our evenings. She lived in a hotel not far from the beach. Pran lived close by with his wife and child but most of his time was spent with Kuldip. One day, Shyam, Taji and I were on our way to a hotel for a glass of beer when we were waylaid by D.N. Madhok, the famous lyricist, who insisted that we go with him to the bar of Eros Cinema. Madhok was Bombay's king of taxis. For instance, the big jalopy waiting for him in the parking lot he had

had in tow for the last three days. After we came out of the bar, Madhok said he was going to visit his current girlfriend, Nigar Sultana, who once used to be Shyam's girlfriend. She lived not far from Kuldip's place. Shyam suggested that we should go and look up Pran, so we all filed into Madhok's taxi, and while he got dropped off at Nigar Sultana's, the driver took us to Kuldip's hotel. Pran was there. He had had a couple because he looked sleepy. Shyam proposed that we should play cards, which might wake up Pran. Kuldip agreed right away but said it would have to be flush and with stakes. Kuldip sat behind Pran, her pointed chin on his shoulder. Every time he won a hand, she would pick up the money. I had often played before, but I had never been in a game like this. Of the money I had, seventy-five rupees was gone in fifteen minutes flat. 'The cards are stacked against me today,' I consoled myself. Shyam said to me, 'That's enough.' Pran smiled and asked Kuldip to return my money.

I said there was no question of that because he had won the money. Pran replied that I should know that he was the best card sharper in town and since I was a friend he could not cheat me. My first thought was that he wanted to return the money to me out of sympathy but when he picked up the pack and dealt it four times in a row, with him holding the highest cards each time, I was convinced that he was right. Pran asked Kuldip to return my money but she refused. Shyam was furious; Pran was not too happy either and he walked out in a huff. He also had to take his wife somewhere. Shyam and I sat for some more time. 'Let's go out,' I suggested. Kuldip was game. We sent for a taxi and took it towards Byculla. I lived by myself on Clare Road but had Shyam staying with me. I took them home. As soon as we entered, Shyam began to flirt with Kuldip. She kept warding him off, but with good humour, because she was not the kind of woman who was easily offended by such things. She knew what she wanted and she had a lot of self-confidence.

I forgot to mention that before we arrived at my place, Kuldip asked the driver to stop at a store as she wanted to buy a perfume. Shyam was angry because she was going to buy the perfume with my money out of which I had been cheated. I told him to forget the whole thing as it was of no consequence. I went into the store with Kuldip. She picked up a bottle for twenty-two rupees eight annas, slipped it into her handbag and told me to pay. I did not want to, but the store owner knew me and the way she had asked me to pay ensured that I would do so out of male vanity. I paid. When Shyam learnt what had happened, he was even angrier. He abused both Kuldip and me but cooled down after some time. He still had hopes of Kuldip. I put in a word for him as well and she appeared to soften. I offered to leave them alone so that they could work out the details of their new 'agreement', but Shyam said it would have to be finalized at her hotel. The taxi was still down there, waiting, so they took it. I was pleased that at least something had worked out.

Shyam was back within thirty minutes and he looked angry. I poured him a brandy and noticed that he had an injured hand. 'What happened?' I asked. It turned out that Kuldip had taken him to the hotel where she lived, but contrary to what he thought she wanted, she had asked him to leave. In frustration, he had tried to hit her, but she had moved and he had hit the wall instead. She had burst out laughing and left the room, leaving Shyam with injured male pride and a bleeding hand.

Some years after Independence, there was a story in the papers that Kuldip had been charged with spying for Pakistan. I have no idea if there was any truth in that report but I felt that a woman like Kuldip Kaur who was utterly straightforward could never be a Mata Hari.

NARGIS: NARCISSUS OF
THE UNDYING BLOOM

It was a long time ago. The Nawab of Chattari's daughter Tasnim—later Mrs Tasnim Saleem Chattari—had written me a letter: 'So what do you think of your brother-in-law, my husband? Since his return from Bombay, he has been talking ceaselessly about you, much to my delight. He was apprehensive of meeting you, my unseen, unmet brother. In fact, he used to tease me about you. Now for the last two days he has been insisting that I should come to Bombay and meet you. He says you are a fascinating person. The way he talks about you, it would seem that you are his brother rather than mine . . . in any case, he is very happy that I choose people carefully. My own brother got here before Saleem did and lost no time in telling me of his meeting with you. Nargis he never mentioned, but when Saleem arrived and spilled the beans, including your fracas with Nakhshab, only then did everything fall into place. Saleem is apologetic about the second visit to Jaddan Bai's house and holds his brother Shamshad, whom you have met, responsible for it . . . You do know, of course, that if Saleem was ever infatuated, it was with Leela Chitnis, which, at least, shows good taste.'

When Saleem dropped in to see me in Bombay, it was our first meeting, and he already was, as Tasnim put it, my brother-in-law, being her husband. I showed him what hospitality I could. Movie people have one 'present' they can always give: take their visitors to see a film being shot. So, dutifully, I took him around to Shri Studio where K. Asif was shooting *Phool*.

Saleem and his friends should have been happy with that but it appeared to me that they had other plans, which they obviously had made before arriving in Bombay. So at one point, quite casually, Saleem asked me, 'And where is Nargis these days?'

'With her mother,' I replied lightly. My joke fell flat because one of the nawabs asked with the utmost simplicity, 'With Jaddan Bai?'

'Yes.'

Saleem spoke next, 'Can one meet her . . . I mean my friends here are quite keen on doing that. Do you know her?'

'I do . . . but only just,' I answered.

'Why?' one of them asked.

'Because she and I have never worked on a movie together,' I said.

'Then we should really not bother you with this,' Saleem remarked.

However, I did want to visit Nargis. I had decided to do so several times but I had not been able to bring myself to go there. These young men whom I would be taking to see her were the kind who just stare at women with their eyes practically jumping out of their sockets. But they were an innocent lot. All they wanted was to catch a glimpse of Nargis so that when they went back to their lands and estates they would be able to brag to their friends that they had met Nargis, the famous film star. So I told them that we could go and meet her.

Why did I want to meet Nargis? After all, Bombay was full of actresses to whose homes I could go any time I wished. Before I answer that question, let me narrate an interesting story.

I was at Filmistan and my working day was long, starting early and ending at eight in the evening. One day, I returned earlier than usual, in fact, in the afternoon, and as I entered my place, I felt there was something different about it, as if someone had strummed a stringed instrument and then disappeared from view. Two of my wife's younger sisters were doing their hair but they seemed to be preoccupied. Their lips were moving but I couldn't hear a word. It was obvious they were trying to hide something. I eased myself into a sofa and the two sisters, after whispering in each other's ears, said in chorus, 'Bhai, salaam.' I answered the greeting, then looked at them intently and asked, 'What is the matter?' I thought they were planning to go to the movies but it was not so. They consulted one another, again in whispers, burst out laughing and ran into the next room. I was convinced they had invited a friend of theirs and since I had come in unexpectedly I had upset their plans.

The three sisters were together for some time and I could hear them talking. There was much laughter. After a few minutes, my wife, pretending that she was talking to her sisters but actually wishing me to pay attention, said, 'Why are you asking me? Why don't you talk to him? Saadat, you are unusually early today.' I told her there was no work at the studio. 'What do these girls want?' I asked. 'They want to say that they are expecting Nargis,' she answered. 'So what? Hasn't she been here before?' I replied, quite sure they were talking about a Parsi girl who lived in the neighbourhood and often visited them. Her mother was married to a Muslim. 'This Nargis has never been here before. I am talking of Nargis the actress,' my wife replied. 'What is she going to do here?' I asked.

My wife then told me the entire story. There was a telephone in the house and the three sisters loved to be on it whenever they had a minute. When they got tired of talking to their friends, they would dial an actress's number and carry on a generally nonsensical conversation with her, such as, 'Oh! We are great fans of yours. We have arrived from Delhi only today and with great difficulty we have been able to get your phone number . . . We are dying to meet you . . . We would have come but we are in purdah and cannot leave the house . . . You are so lovely, absolutely ravishing and what a wonderfully sweet voice you are gifted with—' although they knew that the voice which was heard on the screen was that of either Amir Bai Karnatiki or Shamshad Begum.

Actresses had unlisted numbers; otherwise their phones would never have stopped ringing. But these three had managed to get almost everyone's number with the help of my friend the screenwriter Agha Khalish Kashmiri. During one of their phone sessions, they had called Nargis and they liked the way she talked to them. They were the same age and so they became friends and would talk on the phone often, but they were yet to meet.

Initially, the sisters did not let on who they were. One would say she was from Africa while the other was from Lucknow who was here to meet her aunt. Or she was from Rawalpindi and had travelled to Bombay just to catch a glimpse of Nargis. My wife would at times pretend to be a woman from Gujarat, at others, a Parsi. Quite a few times, Nargis would ask them in exasperation to tell her who they really were and why they were hiding their real names.

It was obvious that Nargis liked them, although there could have been no shortage of fans phoning her home. These three girls were different and she was dying to know who they really were because she did very much want to meet them. Whenever these three mysterious ones called, she would drop everything and talk to them for hours. One day, Nargis insisted that they should meet. My wife told her where we lived, adding that if there was any difficulty in locating the place she should phone from a hotel in Byculla and they would come and get her. When I came home that day, Nargis had just phoned to say that she was in the area but could not find the house, so they were all getting ready in desperation to fetch her. I had entered at a very awkward time.

The two younger sisters were afraid I would be annoyed, while my wife was just nervous. I wanted to pretend I was annoyed but it did not seem right. It was just an innocent prank. Was my wife behind this madcap scheme or was it her sisters'? It is said in Urdu that one's sister-in-law owns half the household and here I was, not with one but two. I offered to go out and fetch Nargis. As I walked out of the door, I heard loud clapping from the other room.

In the main Byculla square, I saw Jaddan Bai's huge limousine—and her. We greeted each other. 'Manto, how are you?' Jaddan Bai asked in a rather loud voice. 'I am well, but what are you doing here?' I asked. She looked at her daughter who was in the back seat and said, 'Nothing, except that Baby has to meet some friends but we can't find the house.' I smiled. 'Let me guide you.' When Nargis heard this, she drew her face close to the window. 'Do you know where they live?' 'But of course!' I replied. 'Who can forget his own house!' Jaddan Bai shifted the paan she was chewing from one side of her mouth to the other and said, 'What kind of storytelling is this?' I opened the door and got in next to her. 'Bibi, this is no story, but if it is one, then its authors happen to be my wife and her sisters.' Then I told them everything that had happened since I returned home. Nargis listened with great concentration, but her mother was not so amused. 'A curse be on the devils . . . if they had said at the start that they were calling from your home, I would have sent Baby over right away. My, my, for days we were all so curious . . . By God, you have no idea how excited and worked up Baby has been over these phone calls. Whenever the phone rang, she would run. Every time I would ask her who it was at the other end with whom she had been carrying on such a sweet conversation for hours, and she would reply that she did not know who they were but they sounded very nice. Once or twice, I also picked up the phone and was impressed by their good manners. They seemed to be from a nice family. But the imps would not tell me their names. Today Baby was beside herself with joy because they had invited her to their place and told her where they lived. I said to her, "Are you mad? You don't know who they are." But she just would not listen and kept after me, so I had to come myself. Had I known by God that these goblins lived in your house—'

'Then you would not have come personally.' I did not let her complete her sentence.

A smile appeared on her face. 'Of course, don't I know you?'

Jaddan Bai was well read and always read my writings. Only recently, one of my pieces, 'The Graveyard of the Progressives', had appeared in *Saqi*, the Urdu literary magazine edited by Shahid Ahmad Dehlvi. God knows why, but she now turned to that. 'By God, Manto, what a writer you are! You can really put the knife in, as you did in that one. Baby, do you remember how I kept raving about that article for the rest of the day?'

But Nargis was thinking of her unseen friends. 'Let's go, bibi,' she implored her mother impatiently.

'Let's go then,' Jaddan Bai said to me.

We were home in minutes. The three sisters saw us from the

upstairs balcony. The younger two just could not contain their excitement and were continually whispering in each other's ears. We walked up the stairs, and while Nargis and the two girls moved into the next room, Jaddan Bai, my wife and I sat in the front room. We amused ourselves by going over the charade the girls had been playing all these months. My wife, now feeling calmer, got down to playing the hostess while Jaddan Bai and I talked about the movie industry and the state it was in. She always carried her paandaan with her because she could not be without her paan, which gave me an opportunity to help myself to a couple as well.

I had not seen Nargis since she was ten or eleven years old. I remembered her holding her mother's hand on movie opening nights. She was a thin-legged girl with an unattractive long face and two unlit eyes. She seemed to have just woken up or about to go to sleep. But now she was a young woman and her body had filled out in all the right places, though her eyes were the same—small, dreamy, even a bit sickly. I thought she had been given an appropriate name, Nargis, the narcissus. In Urdu poetry, the narcissus is always said to be ailing and sightless.

She was simple and playful like a child and was always blowing her nose as if she had a perennial cold; this was used in the movie *Barsaat* as an endearing habit. Her wan face indicated that she had acting talent. She was in the habit of talking with her lips slightly joined. Her smile was self-conscious and carefully cultivated. One could see that she would use these mannerisms as raw material to forge her acting style. Acting, come to think of it, is made up of just such things.

Another thing that I noticed about her was her conviction that one day she would become a star, though she appeared to be in no hurry to bring that day closer. She did not want to bid farewell quite yet to the small joys of girlhood and move into the larger, chaotic world of adults with its working life.

But back to that afternoon. The three girls were now busy exchanging their experiences of convent schools and home. They had no interest right now in what happened in movie studios or how love affairs took place. Nargis had forgotten that she was a film star who captivated many hearts when she appeared on the screen. The two girls were equally unconcerned with the fact that Nargis was an actress who was sometimes shown doing rather daring things in the movies.

My wife, who was older than Nargis, had already taken her under her wing as if she were another of her younger sisters. Initially, she was interested in Nargis because she was a film actress who fell in love with different men in her movies, who laughed and cried or danced as required by the script, but not now. She seemed to be more concerned about her eating sour things, drinking ice-cold water or working in too many films as it could affect her health. It was perfectly all right with her that Nargis was an actress.

While the three of us were busy chatting, in walked a relation of mine whom we all called Apa Saadat. Not only was she my namesake, but also a most flamboyant personality, a person who was totally informal, so much so that I did not even feel the need to introduce her to Jaddan Bai. She lowered herself, all two hundred plus pounds of her, on to the sofa and said, 'Saffo jaan, I pleaded with your brother not to buy this excuse for a car but he just wouldn't listen. We had only driven a few yards when the dashed thing came to a stop and there he is now trying to get it going. I told him that I was not going to stand there but was taking myself to your place to wait.'

Jaddan Bai had been talking of some dissolute nawab, a topic Apa Saadat immediately pounced on. She knew all the nawabs and other rulers of the states that dotted the Kathiawar region because her husband belonged to the ruling family of the Mangrol state. Jaddan Bai knew all those princes because of her profession. The conversation at one point turned to a well known courtesan who had the reputation of having bankrupted several princely states. Apa Saadat was in her element. 'God protect us from these women. Whosoever falls into their clutches is lost both to this world and the next. You can say goodbye to your money, your health and your good name if you get ensnared by one of these creatures. The biggest curse in the world, if you ask me, is these courtesans and prostitutes . . .'

My wife and I were severely embarrassed and did not know how to stop Apa Saadat. Jaddan Bai, on the other hand, was agreeing with all her observations with the utmost sincerity. Once or twice, I tried to interrupt Apa Saadat but she got even more carried away. For a few minutes she heaped every choice abuse on 'these women'. Then suddenly she paused, her fair and broad face underwent a tremor or two and the tiny diamond ornament in her nose sparkled even more than it normally did. She slapped herself on the thigh and stammered, looking at Jaddan Bai, 'You, you are Jaddan. You are Jaddan Bai, aren't you?'

'Yes,' Jaddan Bai replied soberly.

Apa Saadat did not stop. 'Oh you, I mean, you are a very high-class courtesan, isn't that so Saffo jaan?' My wife froze. I looked at Jaddan Bai and gave her a smile, which must have been a sheepish one. Jaddan Bai did not flinch, but calmly and in great detail continued her story of this most notorious courtesan. However, the situation could not be recovered. Apa Saadat had finally realized her faux pas and we were too embarrassed to say anything. Then the girls walked in and the tension evaporated. When Nargis was asked to sing, Jaddan Bai told us, 'I did not teach her to sing because Mohan Babu was not in favour of it, and the truth is I too was against it. She can sing a bit though.' Then she said to her daughter, 'Baby, sing something.'

Like a child, Nargis began to sing. She had no voice at all. It was not sweet nor was the timbre good. Compared to her, my youngest sister-in-law was a thousand times better. However, since Nargis had been asked and asked repeatedly, we had to suffer her for two or three minutes. When she finished, everyone praised her, except Apa Saadat and I. After a few minutes Jaddan Bai said it was time to go. The girls embraced one another and promised to meet again. There was much whispering. Then mother and daughter were gone.

This was my first meeting with Nargis.

I met her several times after this. The telephone was kept busy; the girls would phone her and she would get into her car without her mother and come over. The feeling that she was an actress had almost disappeared. The girls met as if they were related or had known one another for years. Many times, after she had left, the three sisters would say, 'There is nothing actress-like about her.'

A new movie starring Nargis was released around this time with quite a few love scenes which showed her whispering coyly to the hero, looking at him longingly, nuzzling up to him, holding his hand and so on. My wife said, 'Look at her, the way she is sighing, one would think she really was in love with this fellow.' Her two sisters would say to each other, 'Only yesterday she was asking us how to make toffee with raw sugar and here she is . . .'

My own view of Nargis's acting abilities was that she was incapable of portraying emotion. Her inexperienced fingers could not possibly feel the racing pulse of love. Nor could she be aware of the excitement of love, which was different from the excitement of running a race in school. Any perceptive viewer could see from her early movies that her acting was untouched by artifice or deception. The most effective artifice must appear to be natural, but since Nargis was callow and inexperienced, her performances were totally artless. It was only her sincerity and her love for the profession that carried her through her early movies. She was naive about the ways of the world and some of that genuine innocence came through in her performance. Since then, given age and experience, she has become a mature actress. She knows well the difference between love and the games she played at school. She can portray all the nuances of love. She has come of age.

It is good that her journey to acting fame was a slow one. Had she arrived there in one leap, it would have hurt the artistic feelings of perceptive filmgoers. If her off-screen life in her early years had been anything like the roles she was given to play, I for one would have died of shock.

Nargis could have become only an actress, given the fact of her birth. Jaddan Bai was getting on and, though she had two sons, her entire concentration was on Baby Nargis, a plain-looking girl who could not sing. However, Jaddan Bai knew that a sweet voice could be borrowed, and if one had the talent even the disadvantage of ordinary looks could be surmounted.

That was why she had devoted herself entirely to Nargis's development and ensured that whatever talent her daughter had was fully brought out and made central to her personality. Nargis was destined to become an actress and she did become one. The secret of her success, in my opinion, was her sincerity, a quality she always retained. In Jaddan Bai's family there was Mohan Babu, Baby Nargis and her two brothers. All of them were the responsibility of Jaddan Bai. Mohan Babu came from a rich family and had been so fascinated with the musical web Jaddan Bai's mellifluous voice had woven around him that he had allowed her to become his entire life. He was handsome and he had money. He was also an educated man and enjoyed good health. All these assets he had laid at her feet like offerings in a temple. Jaddan Bai enjoyed great fame at the time. Rajas and nawabs would shower her with gold and silver when she sang. However, after this rain of gold and silver was over, she would put her arms around Mohan because he was all she really cared about. He stayed by her side until the end and she loved him deeply. He was also the father of her children. She had no illusions about rajas and nawabs; she knew that their money smelt of the blood of the poor. She also knew that when it came to women, they were capricious.

Nargis was always conscious that my sisters-in-law, whom she came to meet, and spent hours with, were different from her. She was always reluctant to invite them to her home, afraid that they might say it was not possible for them to accept her invitation. One day when I was not around, she told her friends, 'Now you must come to my home some time.' The sisters looked at one another, not sure what to say. Since my wife was aware of my views, she accepted Nargis's invitation, but she did not tell me. All three went.

Nargis had sent them her car and when it arrived at Marine Drive, Bombay's most luxurious residential area, they realized that Nargis had made special arrangements for them. Mohan Babu and his two grown-up sons had been asked not to stay around because Nargis was expecting her friends. The male servants were not allowed into the room where the women were.

Jaddan Bai came in for a few minutes, exchanged greetings and left. She did not want to inhibit them in any way. All three sisters kept saying later how excited Nargis was by their presence in her home. Elaborate arrangements had been made and special milk shakes had been ordered from the nearby Parisian Dairy. Nargis had gone herself to get the drinks because she did not trust a servant to get the right thing. In her excitement and enthusiasm, she broke a glass, which was part of a new set. When her guests expressed regret, she said, 'It's nothing. Bibi will be annoyed but daddy will quieten her down and the matter will be forgotten.'

After the milk shakes, Nargis showed them her albums of photographs, which had stills from many of her movies. There was a world of difference between the Nargis who was showing them the pictures and the Nargis who was the subject of those pictures. Off and on, the three sisters would look at her to compare her with the movie photographs. 'Nargis, how do you become Nargis?' one of them asked. Nargis merely smiled. My wife told me that at home Nargis was simple, homely and childlike, not the bouncing, flirtatious girl whom people saw on the screen. I always felt a sadness floating in her eyes like an unclaimed body in the still waters of a pond whose surface is occasionally disturbed by the breeze.

It was clear to me that Nargis would not have to wait long for the fame which was her destiny. Fate had already taken a decision and handed her the papers, signed and sealed. Why then did she look sad? Did she perhaps feel in an unconscious way that this make-believe game of love she played on the screen would one day lead her to a desert where she would see nothing but mirage followed by mirage, where her throat would be parched with thirst and the clouds would have no rain to release? The sky would offer no solace, and the earth would suck in all moisture deep into its recesses because it would not believe she was thirsty. In the end, she herself would come to believe that her thirst was an illusion.

Many years have passed and when I see her on the screen, I find that her sadness has turned into melancholy. In the beginning, one felt that she was searching for something but now even that urge has been overtaken by despondency and exhaustion. Why? This is a question only Nargis could answer.

But back to the three sisters at Nargis's house. Since they had gone there on their own, they did not stay long. The two younger ones were afraid I would find out and be annoyed, so they took Nargis's leave and came home. I noticed that whenever they talked about Nargis, it would come to the question of marriage. The younger ones were dying to know when or whom she would marry, while my wife, who had been married for five years, would speculate about what kind of mother Nargis would make.

My wife did not tell me at first about their visit, but when she did I pretended to be displeased. She was immediately on the defensive and agreed that it was a mistake. She wanted me to keep it to myself because, according to the moral and social milieu in which the three had been brought up, visiting the home of an actress was improper. As far as I know, they had not told even their mother that they had gone to see Nargis, although the old lady was by no means narrow-minded. To this day, I do not understand why they thought they had done something wrong. What was wrong with going to see Nargis at her home? Why was acting considered a bad profession? Did we not have people in our own family who had spent their entire lives telling lies and practising hypocrisy? Nargis was a professional actress. What she did, she did in the open. It was not she but others who practised deception.

Since I began this account with Tasnim Saleem Chattari's letter, let me return to it because that is what set the whole thing off. Since I was keen to meet Nargis at her own place, I went along with Saleem and his friends despite being busy. The correct thing would have been to phone Jaddan Bai to see if Nargis was free or not, but since in my daily life I was no great believer in such formalities, I just appeared at her door. Jaddan Bai was sitting on her veranda, slicing betel nut. As soon as she saw me, she said in a loud voice, 'Oh! Manto, come in, come in.' Then she shouted for Nargis, 'Baby, your sahelis are here,' thinking that I had brought my two sisters-in-law. When I told her that I was accompanied not by sahelis but sahelas, and also who they were, her tone changed. 'Call them in,' she said. When Nargis came running out, she said to her, 'Baby, you go in, Manto sahib has his friends with him.' She received Saleem and his companions as if they were buyers who had come to inspect the house. The informality with which she always spoke to me had disappeared. Instead of 'Sit down', it was 'Do please make yourselves comfortable', and 'Want a drink?' had become 'And what would you prefer for a drink?' I felt like a fool.

When I told her the purpose of our visit, her rather studied and stylized reply took me aback. 'Oh! They want to meet Baby? The poor thing has been down with a bad cold for days. Her heavy work schedule has taken the last ounce of energy out of her. I tell her every day, "Daughter, just rest for a day." But she does not listen, so devoted is she to her work. Even director Mehboob has told her the same thing, offering to suspend the shooting for a day, but it has no effect on her. Today, I put my foot down because her cold was bad. Poor thing!'

Naturally, my young friends were gravely disappointed when they heard that. They had caught a glimpse of her from the taxi when she had briefly run on to the veranda, but they were dying to see her from close quarters and were disappointed that she was ill. Jaddan Bai, meanwhile, had begun to talk of other things and I could see that my young friends were bored. Since I knew there was nothing the matter with Nargis, I said to Jaddan Bai, 'I know it is going to be hard on Baby but they have come from so far; maybe she could come in for a minute.'

After being summoned three or four times, Nargis finally appeared. All of them stood up and greeted her in a very courtly manner. I did not rise. Nargis had made the entry of an actress. Her conversation too was that of an actress, as if she were delivering her given lines. It was quite silly. 'It is such a great pleasure to meet you'. 'Yes, we only arrived in Bombay today'. 'Yes, we will be returning the day after'. 'You are now the top star of India'. 'We have always seen the opening show of every one of your movies'. 'The picture you have given us will go into our album'. Mohan Babu also joined us at one point but he did not say a word, just kept looking at us with his big eyes before going into some reverie of his own.

Jaddan Bai spoke most of the time, making it clear to her visitors that she was personally acquainted with every Indian raja and nawab. Nargis's entire conversation was pure artifice. The way she sat, the way she moved, the way she raised her eyes, was like an offering on a platter. Obviously, she expected them to respond in the same self-conscious, artificial manner. It was a boring and somewhat tense meeting. The young men felt inhibited in my company, as I did in theirs. It was interesting to see a different Nargis from the one to whom I was accustomed. Saleem and his friends went to see her again the next day, but without telling me. Perhaps this meeting was different. As for my argument with the poet Nakhshab to which Tasnim Saleem had referred in her letter, I do not have the least recollection of it. It is possible he was there when we arrived because Jaddan Bai was fond of poetry and liked to entertain poets and have them recite. It is possible I may have had a tiff with Nakhshab.

I saw another aspect of Nargis's personality once when I was with Ashok. Jaddan Bai was planning to launch a production of her own and wanted Ashok to play the lead, but since Ashok, as usual, did not want to go by himself, he had asked me to come along. During our conversation, we discussed many things but discreetly, things such as business, money, flattery and friendship. At times, Jaddan Bai would talk as a senior, at others as the movie producer and at times as Nargis's mother who wanted the right price paid for her daughter's work. Mohan Babu would nod his agreement now and then.

They were talking big money, money which was going to be spent, money which had been spent. However, each paisa was carefully discussed and accounted for. Nargis was pretty businesslike. She seemed to suggest, 'Look Ashok, I agree that you are a polished actor and famous but I am not to be undermined. You will have to concede that I can be your equal in acting.' This was the point she wanted to hammer home. Off and on, the woman in her would come to life, as if she were telling Ashok, 'I know there are thousands of girls who are in love with you, but I too have thousands of admirers and if you don't believe that, ask anyone . . . maybe you too will become my admirer one of these days.'

Periodically, Jaddan Bai would play the conciliator. 'Ashok, the world is crazy about you and Baby, so I want the two of you to appear together. It will be a sensation and we will all be happy.' Sometimes, she would address me. 'Manto, Ashok has become such a great star and he is such a nice man, so quiet, so shy. God grant him a long life! For this movie, I have had a role specially written for him. When I tell you all about it, you will be thrilled.'

I did not know what role or character she had got specially written for Ashok, but anyway I was happy for her. It did occur to me though that Jaddan Bai herself was playing a most fascinating role, and the one she had chosen for Nargis was even more fascinating. Had this been a scene being shot with Ashok, she could not have spoken her lines with more conviction. At one point, Suraiya's name came up and she pulled a long face and started saying nasty things about her family and pulling her down as if she were doing it out of a sense of duty. She said Suraiya's voice was bad, she could not hold a note, she had had no musical training, her teeth were bad and so on. I am sure had someone gone to Suraiya's home, he would have witnessed the same kind of surgery being performed on Nargis and Jaddan Bai. The woman whom Suraiya called her grandmother, but who was actually her mother, would have taken a drag at her hookah and told even nastier stories about Jaddan Bai and Nargis. I know that whenever Nargis's name came up, Suraiya's mother would look disgusted and compare her face to a rotting papaya.

Mohan Babu's big, handsome eyes have been eternally closed for many years and Jaddan Bai has been lying under tons of earth for a long time, her heart full of unrequited desires. As for her Baby Nargis, she stands at the top of that make-believe ladder we know as the movies, though it is hard to say if she is looking up, or if she is looking down at the first rung on which she put her tiny child's foot many years ago. Is she seeking a patch of dark under those brilliant arc lights that illuminate her life now, or is she searching for a tiny ray of light in that darkness? This interplay of light and dark constitutes life, although in the world of movies there are times when the dividing line between the two ceases to exist.

SITARA: THE DANCING TIGRESS FROM NEPAL

As a writer, I have had to go through and overcome many difficulties, but I have never felt more hesitant than I do now as I sit down to record my memories of the famous dancer and film star Sitara. To most, she was known as an actress who was a superb dancer, but I happened to have the opportunity to study her character, hence this piece. Sitara was a living case history, and only a psychologist could write about her as she deserved to be written about. Over the years, I have known and analysed many women but the more I learnt about her, the closer I came to the view that she was not a woman but a typhoon which did not blow in and out as typhoons do, but which retained its force and fury without showing any signs of weakening. She may have been a woman of average build but she was stronger than most people I have known. Had another woman suffered as many illnesses as she did, she could not have survived. Sitara was made of a different clay and was both brave and strong-minded. She never missed her morning dance exercises and spent at least an hour dancing as if there was no tomorrow.

Every morning, she would dance with bone-breaking vigour for an hour, but I never found her looking tired. She had amazing stamina and there was never a sign of fatigue on her face. She loved her art in the same total way as she loved her men. Even for an ordinary performance, she would rehearse for hours and give it everything she had. She always wanted to do new things. Her movements were swift and she was one of those restless people who cannot sit still even for a minute. She was always up and about.

She had two sisters, Tara and Alaknanda, which made them

a female trinity. These three sisters were probably born in a Nepalese village and came to Bombay one by one to seek their fortune. Her sisters faded out long ago and there would be few who would even recall their names, but in their time they had lived interesting lives. Tara had many affairs, including one with Shaukat Hashmi who was married to Purnima who later divorced him. Alaknanda passed through many hands and in the end settled down with the famous Prabhat Studio actor Balwant Singh. How long she lived with him, I do not know. Of the three sisters, only Sitara was able to make a mark. I hesitate to write about her because she was not one but several women, and so many were the men with whom she had affairs that it would be impossible to deal with them all in one short piece.

Were the sisters to have a biographer, the book would run into thousands of pages. I have often been denounced as a writer of pornography. Those who do so never give me credit for refusing to write about smutty people, and God knows there are enough of them in this world. People, in my view, do smutty things either out of instinct or because of the surroundings in which they live. What comes instinctively to a human being can perhaps be kept under control if he tries, but if he is indifferent, then whom can he blame except himself?

Whenever I think of Sitara, I am reminded of a typical five-storey Bombay high-rise with many flats and rooms, all inhabited. It is a fact that she had the ability to be involved with many men at the same time. When she came to Bombay, she was with a gaunt-looking Gujarati film director whose name I do not recall but it was some Desai. They were probably married too. He was very good at his work but obstinate by nature, which earned him many rejections. I met him at a time when Saroj Film Company was still in business but dying slowly. We became friends right away because he understood film-making and had a taste for literature. Sitara had just left him but he had few regrets because he told me that he did not have the ability to cope with a woman like her. She then lived with someone else but, off and on, she would come to see Desai. He would welcome her but never encourage her to stay long. There was no divorce under Hindu law. Desai and Sitara had had a Hindu marriage and, despite her affairs with a succession of men, technically she remained Mrs Desai.

I am taking you back to the time when Mehboob's star was rising. He cast her in one of his movies and soon there was a roaring affair going on between the two of them. I won't write about it because only Ishrat Jahan—known to movie-goers as Bibbo—can do justice to this story. Mehboob was shooting outdoors in Hyderabad and, despite his affair with Sitara, his routine was unchanged. He would offer his prayers with the greatest devotion and make love to her with the same single-minded enthusiasm. Mehboob was completing a movie at Film City Studio where P.N. Arora (later to make his mark as a producer) was the sound recordist. Fazalbhai who was all-in-all at Film City, had earlier sent Arora to England for training. The recording laboratory was under the overall charge of Seth Shiraz Ali. Mehboob was still carrying on with Sitara. But according to Diwan Singh Maftoon, editor of the famous journal *Riasat*, she was also having it on the side with Arora. After the Mehboob movie was done, she moved in with Arora. Then there appeared on the scene the handsome Al-Nasir who had just arrived from Dehra Dun to become an actor. Because of his looks, he was given a role in a movie which also starred Sitara. It was only to be expected that he would get added to her list. In effect, besides Al-Nasir, she was maintaining relations with three other men all more or less simultaneously: her husband Desai, Arora and Mehboob.

Her fifth man was Nazir whose mistress, a Jewish actress by the name of Yasmin, had recently left him. I don't know exactly how Nazir and Sitara met, but they instantaneously fell for each other. Nazir was a very forthcoming and open-hearted person. When we met, for instance, instead of shaking hands, he would shower me with the choicest abuse, his way of showing affection. He had a heart of gold and he was straight as an arrow. His affair with Sitara lasted for several years. Because of his strong personality, she temporarily gave up the other men but it was not going to last because Sitara was not a one-man woman. Before long, she had fallen into her old ways with time for everybody: Arora, Al-Nasir, Mehboob and her husband. This was too much for a self-respecting man like Nazir who believed in maintaining a relationship faithfully, once it had been formed. Sitara was made of different clay and even a man like Nazir could not keep her from hopping into bed with other men. His former mistress Yasmin was both very feminine and quite beautiful, but when she told Nazir that she would like to settle down with a husband and home, he, whom many considered a hard man, had said to her in all sincerity that, since they were not going to get married, she was free to marry whom she pleased. How that kind of a person could carry on with a woman like Sitara for so long always baffled me.

I first met Nazir at Hindustan Cinetone. It was a bad time for the movie industry. Many financiers had become bankrupt because of playing the stock market to make quick money. The original name of Cinetone used to be Saroj Film Company, and God knows what else before that. I had written a story called *Keechar*, which Seth Nanoobhai Desai had liked immensely. It was the sort of story that no producer would have been willing to film because of its theme, which was sure to provoke the government's ire. Nanoobhai was a brave man and he had bought my story, but the project had remained incomplete because of other difficulties he had run into. I had specially written a character—that of a labourer—for Nazir, which he had liked. On learning that Nanoobhai was unable to make that 'heretical' film, he had offered to buy the story and promised to film it no matter what it took. Since Nanoobhai really liked the story, he had declined the offer. He had also in the meantime arranged the money, and the film, which was in the Gujarati language, was directed by Dad Gunjal, completed and released. Nazir had been playing with the idea of forming a film company of his own for some time and, being at a loose end since the end of his affair with Yasmin, he had concentrated on this project and managed to set it up. As far as I can remember, his first production was *Sandesa*, followed by *Society*, which starred Sitara. And that was when she had really got him under her spell though, true to form, she had not stopped meeting her other lovers, especially P.N. Arora.

Here is an interesting story. After I left Bombay for a year to work for All India Radio in Delhi, it was only natural that I would remain largely unaware of the gossip in Bombay. One day I ran into Arora on the street. He was walking with the help of a stick and his back was bent. He had always been thin but he looked in extremely poor shape that day. I felt that he had difficulty even walking, as if there were no life left in him. I was in a tonga and I asked the driver to stop. Expressing surprise at his appearance, I asked him what was wrong. Almost out of breath with fatigue, he managed a faint smile and replied. 'Sitara . . . Manto, Sitara.'

Al-Nasir, who lost his slim, upright and handsome figure after a few years, and became fat and flabby, was a sensation when he first came, with his fair, almost pink complexion, nurtured by the cool hill air of his native Dehra Dun. He was so good-looking that one could almost compare him to a beautiful woman. When I returned to Bombay from Delhi after accepting an offer from Shaukat Hussain Rizvi, I met him at Minerva Movietone. I just could not believe my eyes. His pink complexion had become ashen and his clothes hung loose on him. He seemed to have shrunk, and all energy and strength appeared to have been squeezed out of him. 'My dear, what have you done to yourself?' I asked because I was worried about his health. He whispered the answer in my ear, 'Sitara . . . my dear, Sitara.'

Sitara was everywhere. I wondered if Sitara's only purpose in life was to infect men with pallor, from the England-trained Arora to the Dehra-Dun-born Al-Nasir. So I took Al-Nasir aside and asked him to give me the lowdown on her. He said it was Sitara who had drained him out, and he had come to a point where he knew that if he did not fight free of her and run it would be the end of him. So one day, he had just hopped on a train bound for Dehra Dun where he had spent three months in a sanatorium and recovered some of his strength. He said she had been writing him long letters in Hindi, which he was unable to read, but added that he dreaded their arrival. He again whispered in my ear, 'Manto sahib, that woman . . . I tell you!'

Women like Sitara are rare, perhaps one in a million. She survived illnesses so dangerous that few other women could have scraped through them. She had determination, and so formidable was her constitution that not once, but several times, she successfully cheated death. Many thought that after such grave bouts with a host of ailments, she would lose her will and ability to dance, but they were wrong. She danced as she had always danced, in her later years as in her early youth, giving it everything she had. She would never miss her daily practice and she would have herself massaged every day. She always had two house servants, a man and a woman. The man always performed the massage. As for the woman, she invariably chose one who looked like an old-fashioned procuress.

Sitara was mostly to be seen in a fine muslin sari, which left nothing to the imagination. It wasn't too pretty a sight. She never talked much but she had sharp eyes that noticed everything. When she was fifty-five, she had the agility of an eagle-eyed young woman. For a time she lived alone in Dadar's Khodadad Circle. Khodadad in Urdu means God-given and the truth is that her talent and her qualities were God-given. Nazir, who later got tied up with the actress Swaran Lata (whom he married), despite his tolerance and generosity, could only take so much of Sitara and no more. In the end, he gave up on her because she could never be satisfied with one man. I am told that he had once stood in front of her with his hands joined together in supplication and begged her, 'Sitara, please let me go. I made a mistake and I am sorry for it and I want you to forgive me.'

Nazir used to rough up Sitara occasionally but she did not seem to mind. Perhaps she was one of those women who derive sexual pleasure from this sort of thing. There is an interesting sub-plot to the Sitara–Nazir affair. His nephew K. Asif (later to become a film-maker of note) was staying with his uncle when Sitara was living in the house. Asif was a big, strong man, still tender in years, who, as far as I know, had never known a woman in his life. He was keen on movies and curious to learn everything about them because he had ambition, and he had come to know many film personalities, including actresses, since he had moved in with his uncle. He must also have witnessed what went on between Sitara and Nazir. A restless young man, he was raring to go, and though Sitara may have appeared to him like a stone wall, she was the kind of wall which men like Asif would be challenged to scale.

Nazir's flat was off a courtyard in front of Ranjit Studio. It had three rooms, one of which served as the office of his company, Hind Pictures. The place did not offer much by way of privacy, so it is to be assumed that young Asif must have witnessed, and certainly heard, what a man and a woman do when they are alone. This must have been a new experience for someone whose knowledge of such things consisted of stories he had heard his married friends tell. His opportunity came one day when he actually saw 'action play' between his uncle and his mistress. It reminded him of a fight between two wild dogs who were trying to bite and tear each other apart as, frothing at the mouth, they carried on with their savage encounter. A shiver ran down his spine. Man, he said to himself, was an animal, and love was a deadly encounter, and he wanted to be in just one such encounter himself. His body was young, sinewy and powerful, his blood warm; all he wanted was an opportunity to prove his manhood.

The talented but luckless Pakistani film director Nayyar was also living in Bombay in those days and staying with Nazir. He and Asif were the same age, both bachelors with wild and youthful fantasies. They would talk about women who were to be theirs in the future that stretched ahead. Whenever Sitara's name came up, they would tremble and feel transported to a world inhabited by demonic spirits. They did not know what a nymphomaniac was, nor could they have known that if, on the one hand, there were women like Sitara, the flip side of the coin was that there were others who were frigid like slabs of ice. They did not know then that Sitara was not faithful though she was Nazir's mistress. They did not know that she still made love to Arora, her husband Desai and Al-Nasir. But they did know why every other day there were scratch marks on Nazir's rhinoceros skin.

Sitara would be up at the crack of dawn and begin the day by dancing like a savage for an hour. Her drummer would get exhausted but not she. The earth would tremble under her feet as she completed her exercises. This was followed by an extended session with her masseur. Then she would bathe, put on fresh clothes and go to Nazir who would still be asleep. She would wake him up and make him drink a cup of milk or something else. That over, another dance would begin. Asif and Nayyar were aware of all this. They were still at an age when you look into empty rooms and peek through windows, when the slightest sound makes you come to a standstill, when you try to read a meaning into everything. Nayyar was slightly built compared to Asif and his sexual urges were also less headstrong than his friend's. Asif's body was full of the static of youth and raw passion, which made him long to knock down a woman like a thunderbolt which falls on the earth's stony surface on a dark night.

Sitara would spend hours chatting to Asif. He felt less shy with her than when he had first come from Lahore, but he still could not muster the courage to touch her. He was terrified of his uncle's temper. However, there was one thing he was in no doubt about: Sitara was attracted to him. If he were to grab her wrist, she would come with him, no matter where he took her, even on a bed of stones on a black, stormy night. Asif was restless. He did not want to wait. The two of them were like two trains which are programmed to collide headlong one day. This bothered him because he wanted the collision to take place today. He felt close to her but they were running on parallel tracks, near yet far. There was no physical contact. The two would talk as passengers riding on trains going in opposite directions, only to move apart. Asif was waiting for that dark and stormy night when he would take the leap. Nazir, in the meanwhile, had become suspicious, and he was horrified. One day he screamed at Sitara and ordered her to pack up and leave. He also beat her up.

Sitara was, after all, a woman, and after the violence and unpleasantness with Nazir, she did not have the strength to just walk out of the door. She wanted help, but how could she ask for it? Nazir was frothing at the mouth with anger because he knew what she was up to. That night he went into his office and slept there. Asif knew that his chance had arrived and he slipped into Sitara's room and rubbed her body where it hurt, then he helped her pack and took her to her Khodadad Circle flat in Dadar. Sitara thanked him for his kindness and, encouraged by that, he took her hand and said, 'You don't have to thank me.' She did not try to free it and one thing led to another. And so it came to pass that young Asif joined the long line of men on whom she had cast her siren spell.

Sitara gave him the time of his life. Had it happened during the day, he would have surely seen stars in the sky, but it had taken place at night in the privacy of her flat at Khodadad Circle. Asif was smitten. 'Look,' he said to her, 'we should have a strong relationship; it is time you stopped going with other men. You should belong to just one man.' Sitara promised that she would not look at another man from that day on. Asif was happy and left as he was afraid his uncle might ask him where he had been. He promised to be back the next day. After he left, Sitara went to her dressing table, brushed her hair, put on a fresh sari, walked down to the street, hailed a taxi and gave the driver P.N. Arora's address.

Sitara hated the sight of me. I was editing the film weekly *Mussawar* in which I wrote a couple of satirical but amusing pieces about her. My columns 'Nit Nai' (The Latest) and 'Baal ki Khal' (Splitting Hairs) were popular and always in good taste, but Sitara did not like what I had written; not that I cared because, frankly, there was nothing I wanted from her. It was also my effort, as far as possible, to keep well away from film personalities. When I wrote a rather naughtily embellished account of her quarrel with Nazir, she was beside herself with rage and was said to have abused me all day. When my spies gave me details of her affair with Asif and I made indirect references to it in my columns, she asked him to beat me up, adding that if he didn't she would hire someone to do it. She also asked him to have some other journalist attack me in his paper. Asif did nothing because he could take a joke; he just let Sitara curse me to her heart's content.

Things between Asif and his uncle, meanwhile, had reached a rather delicate stage. Nazir was getting very, very suspicious about his nephew's movements. Asif was out of the house until the small hours and when he was asked where he had been he would come up with one excuse or another. But excuses, no matter how good, run out in the end. Nazir had banished Sitara from his life and once his mind was made up he never changed it. Sitara he did not give a damn about, but he was worried about his nephew whom he had brought all the way from Lahore so that he could make something of himself. He did not want him to fall into Sitara's clutches. He knew her well and he also knew that she fed on young men like Asif. She had a way with men. Most of the time, she did not even have to try; they just fell into her lap willingly and, once there, found all escape routes blocked.

Once a man caught Sitara's fancy, he had to be on call all hours of the day and night. Asif, therefore, had begun to be absent from home much of the time. Once or twice, Nazir asked him if it was Sitara who was the cause of his disappearances. 'Uncle, I wouldn't even think of it,' Asif would say. Not that Nazir believed him. He was too old in tooth and claw not to know that this boy, his own nephew, was Sitara's latest acquisition. As for Asif, had it been a woman other than his uncle's former mistress, he would not have lied; but this was different. How could he tell his uncle that he was having an affair with his ex-mistress? Not only did Asif have no desire whatsoever to turn away from Sitara, he would not even have been able to, had he tried.

Nazir's anger was mounting, but slowly. He did not wish to act until he had caught the two in a compromising position himself. And one day, that opportunity came his way. I do not now remember how Nazir caught Asif, but catch his nephew he did. Asif still swore that there was nothing between Sitara and him, but it was no use. Nazir's first impulse was to break every bone in their bodies, but thanks to the actor Majid (who came to Lahore after 1947), who was in his good books, he cooled down. Majid, on his own, had tried several times to warn Asif about Sitara and the dangerous game he was playing, but Asif was beyond advice. He was also foolish enough to believe that his affair with Sitara would remain a secret. Nazir may have had a temper but he was also a tender-hearted man. He had had a long physical relationship with Sitara. He did not want his nephew to fall into her hands because he knew it would do him no good. Even if Asif had not been his nephew, he would still have given the young man the same advice. Nazir, a man of great sincerity—although he gave the impression of being hard—was not happy with what he had done, rather, not done. And he was nobody's fool; he was perceptive and, what was more, he knew Sitara as few men knew her.

Asif began to get home earlier so as not to provoke his uncle's ire. Once he left, Sitara would make her up face, change and hop into a taxi to spend the rest of the night with Arora on whom the potions of Delhi's herbal medicine miracle-workers had had a salutary effect. He had regained some of his old vigour and he no longer had that hollow-cheeked look. She had not given up on her other old flames either. They—Al-Nasir, Mehboob and God alone knows how many others—remained on her 'active list'. Asif had reduced his visits because of his uncle, but he had not eliminated them. And how could he, even if he had tried. Sitara was like a sorceress of old who turns her lovers into flies and sticks them on the wall. In fairy tales, it always required a prince bearing a special amulet to break the spell and release the sorceress's prisoners. Was a prince going to come to Asif's rescue, because he was bewitched by one on whom even the most potent black magic could not have much effect? She was a fort that could not be stormed; so Asif continued to see Sitara and his relationship with his uncle kept worsening. By the way, after Nazir threw out Sitara, the famous musician Rafiq Ghaznavi had tried to make peace between them but without success. Once he invited Sitara, Arora and Nazir to his flat for drinks but despite his best efforts—he was a most persuasive conversationalist—he could not manage to change Nazir's mind. In the end, everybody left and Sitara spent the night with Rafiq, who kept assuring her that her time with Nazir was a thing of the past and she should accept it. That was the beginning and the end of his peace mission. It was also the first and last night she spent with Rafiq. One wonders why. Was it that he had found her to be less than a perfect dancer and she had discovered that he was not the musician he fancied himself to be?

Sitara was perhaps the first woman in Asif's life and she had taken a shine to him. Nazir, unfortunately, caught them in flagrante delicto one more time, but I do not know who got Asif off the hook this time. Some days later, I heard that Asif had disappeared from Bombay. Then I was told that Sitara was not to be seen anywhere either. When people asked, they were told that she had gone to a Hindu shrine. Had it been the annual Haj pilgrimage season, some wags would have quipped that Asif had gone to the holy land, but it wasn't. Then came the news that both of them were in Delhi, were married, and Sitara had become a Muslim and taken the name Allah Rakhi. One can imagine the effect it must have had on Nazir. Under Hindu personal law there was no divorce. Once a woman was married, she remained married for life. She can have a hundred men but she will remain the wife of the man to whom she first got married. Even if a Hindu woman changes her religion, she remains married to her first husband. From that point of view, Sitara may have become Begum K. Asif; but to all intents and purposes, she was still Mrs Desai.

Once the story was confirmed, I had a field day with it in my *Mussawar* columns. Every week, I would write about the newly-weds in a cutting manner. When the two returned to Bombay after their honeymoon, Nazir was so embarrassed and angry that it is not possible to describe it in words. One day at the races I saw Asif in a sharkskin suit with his arm around Sitara's waist. When he saw me, he smiled, then began to laugh. He shook my hand and said, 'Brilliant, the columns you are writing are most amusing, by God I say.' Sitara made a face and stood aside, but Asif paid no attention to her and kept talking to me for quite some time. He may have had little education but he had the ability to take a joke. In Bombay, the word along the bazaar grapevine was that someone called Asif had married Sitara. In Bhindi Bazaar and Mohammed Ali Road, traditionally Bombay's Muslim-dominated localities, men would sit in Iranian cafes sipping tea and expressing satisfaction over the fact that a Muslim had married a Hindu and converted her to Islam. Most of these devout Muslims often happened to be ardent supporters of the All India Muslim League. Some would say that Asif should not allow this sali to appear in movies; others would say there was nothing wrong with it, as long as she observed purdah when she left home. Some cynics would declare, 'It is all a stunt.' Once I asked Asif if he had really married Sitara in a Muslim ceremony. 'What ceremony, what marriage!' he answered. Only God knows what the truth was.

Asif had no place of his own, so he was living in Sitara's flat and driving her around in her car. In Delhi, Asif had met a financier, Lala Jagat Narayan, and talked him into investing in a movie he wanted to make. He must also have taken an advance because he did not appear to be hard-pressed for funds. Asif had a lot of self-confidence and could get the better even of famous directors and writers. He had great native intelligence, and plenty of horse sense. When he became a director, he did not confine himself to the advice of a small coterie, as so often happens, but invited a cross section of people to advise him, never hesitating to accept a good suggestion or idea.

I am reminded of a story that involves me. When Asif was going to make *Phool* and I was living in a flat on Clare Road, one day I heard persistent honking in the street. I came out on the balcony and found a huge car parked in front of my building. I had a first-floor flat and I bent over to see who the occupant was. It was Asif, who stuck his head out of the car window and smiled. 'Come in,' I said. He opened the car door, said something to Sitara who was in the back seat and replied, 'In a minute.' The car drove off and Asif walked in. He shook hands warmly and said, 'I want to read you my story.' 'I charge a fee as you know,' I said jokingly. Without another word, Asif walked out. I called after him and even ran out to the street but he would not return. All he said was he would come back when he had my fee. I felt ashamed of my bad joke, though I had been quite sure that he would take it in the spirit in which I had made it. When I told my wife what had happened, she said it was silly of me to have said what I had. Asif, after all, was not a close friend and it was understandable that he had reacted the way he had.

Of course, I had not had the least intention of injuring his feelings, nor had I expected him to give me money. On the other hand, I really wanted him to narrate to me the story of his yet-to-be-made film. There were many 'third-class' directors in Bombay who had asked me to listen to their stories not once but twice and even thrice because they wanted my opinion. I had never asked them for money. I regretted having upset Asif. One day, there was a knock at the door. I opened it and found a man with an envelope, which he gave to me, and left. I had not even opened it when I heard a car honk in the road. It was Sitara's car. The envelope contained five hundred rupees and a one-line note, 'Here's the fee. I will come tomorrow.' I was floored. Next day, Asif appeared at nine. 'Well, doctor, have you received your fee?' he asked. I was speechless but I apologized and tried to return the money, but he would not take it. He sank into the sofa and said, 'Manto sahib, what are you thinking? This money is not mine, nor my father's, but the producer's. It was my mistake that I arrived without a fee because I wasn't thinking. I do not believe in getting things done free. You are going to spend your time, so it is only right that you should be paid for it. By God, that is what I believe. But let's forget about this nonsense and let me tell you the story.'

Without giving me an opportunity to answer, he sat down on a sofa and I took a chair facing him. I had never heard him tell a story and it was quite an experience. He rolled up the sleeves of his silk shirt, loosened his belt, pulled up his legs and assumed the classic posture of a yogi. 'Now listen to the story. It is called *Phool*. What do you think of the name?' 'It is good,' I replied. 'Thank you, I will narrate it scene by scene,' he said. Then he began to speak in his typical manner. I do not know who the author was but Asif was playing all the characters, raising his voice, moving around all the time. Now he would be on the sofa, the next minute his back would be against the wall, then he would push his legs against it and his upper torso would be on the floor. At times, he would jump from the sofa on to the floor, only to climb on to a chair the next minute. Then he would stand up straight, looking like a leader asking for votes in an election. It was a long story, like the intestine of the devil, as the expression goes. After he finished his narration, we were silent for a few moments. 'What do you think about it?' Asif asked. 'It is trash,' I replied. Asif bit his lips, sat upright on the sofa and asked furiously, 'What did you say?' Had it been somebody else, that person might have flinched, but I am not made that way. 'It is trash,' I repeated.

Asif tried many of his conjurer's tricks to impress me but they had no effect on me. Also, I simply have no patience with loudness, which was one of Asif's characteristics. Finally, I decided to give it to him. 'Look here, Asif, I suggest you get hold of a big, heavy stone, place it on top of my head and hit that stone with a hammer, once, twice, thrice, and as long as you like. And by God, I swear I would still say that your story is trash.' Asif stood up, took my hand in both of his and said, 'By God, it is trash. I had come only to hear you say that.' I first thought he was joking but he was serious, so we sat down and began to think of improvements.

Asif and Sitara stayed 'married' for quite some time, which reminds me of another story, which predates my friendship with Asif and his relationship with Sitara. Asif had pimples on his face, which are associated with adolescence. I used to think that if youth were so ugly and painful, then may it please God not to bless anyone with youth. (I am thankful to the Almighty that he did confer such youth on me.) I used to dabble in herbal medicine and I wanted to do something for Asif's appearance. I also consulted a couple of doctor friends and one day I brought a handful of medicines for him, but they did him no good. When Sitara came into his life, every pimple on his face disappeared.

Kamal Amrohi and I used to be colleagues at Bombay Talkies. I recall the time when we were trying to put his story, later filmed as *Mahal*, into final shape. One day I noticed a pimple on his face and thought nothing of it, but in a few days it became so painful that we felt something had to be done to rid him of it. 'I have a treatment that can't miss,' I told Kamal. 'What?' he asked. 'Do you know where Sitara lives?' I asked. 'I do,' he replied. 'All you have to do is go there, walk up the stairs right up to her door but under no circumstances are you to enter. There is your cure,' I said. Kamal was an intelligent man and burst out laughing. He knew what I meant.

Meanwhile, Sitara and Asif were living together in Mahim where I visited them several times. Their third-floor flat was at the other end of a street facing the church on Lady Jamshedji Road. Asif had finished *Phool* and was thinking of making *Anarkali*, which Kamal Amrohi had scripted for him, but he was not too happy with it and had asked various people including me to give it a new twist. I used to get to his place by eight in the morning and the door would be answered by an old woman wearing a thin muslin sari, which always made me uneasy. She looked like an old Arabian Nights witch to me. I would go in and sit on the sofa. From the next room, which was the bedroom, I would hear strange noises, which sent a shiver down my spine. After some time, Asif would appear, smacking his lips. He used to be a sight, with his nightshirt torn in various places and blue marks on his chest and arms, his hair dishevelled, and his breathing uneven. He would greet me casually and then fall in a heap on the floor. After some time, Sitara would send him a cup of custard, which he would eat with undisguised reluctance. Then we would begin our work, which was more gossip than anything. The two of them seemed to be doing well, though rumours were spreading that Asif was marrying a girl from his family, that a date had been set, and soon he would be travelling to Lahore with his friends for the ceremony.

I was busy when all this happened; otherwise I would have met him and asked what it was all about. I never got an opportunity until many days later. 'Well, I have decided to put an end to it and I will,' was all he said. He was in a car and I was walking. He had stopped and was in a hurry so we could not have a proper conversation. A few days later, I learnt that Asif had gone to Lahore with a large party of friends and a big wedding had taken place there with drinks flowing and dancing girls performing. Then I heard that Asif had returned to Bombay with his new bride and had rented a portion of a house on Pali Hill, Bandra. I later found out that it was actually Nazir's house and he had vacated one half of it for his nephew. I am not sure what Sitara thought of it, but I do know that her visits to Arora continued. Asif had now begun to make preparations to make *Mughal-e-Azam* (completed several years after Independence).

Then a most interesting development took place. Asif began disappearing from home and it came to light that he was again spending his nights with Sitara. Consequently, the new marriage failed. Nazir's grown-up son was also around at the time and one is not sure what exactly happened, but this much was known that Asif had stopped going home at night. There was much unpleasantness and then we heard that a divorce was in the offing. All through this crisis, Asif kept meeting Sitara. It seemed they were together again. There were many stories in the market about Asif's new wife but I have no wish to go into them because I am not sure if they were true. All I know is that Asif had married in Lahore with great fanfare and brought his bride to Bombay, settled down on Pali Hill and, in less than three months, the marriage was on the rocks. Who but Sitara could have been responsible for it? She was a woman of experience and knew how to make herself attractive to a man, rendering him useless for other women. That was how she had weaned Asif away from his new bride and that was why he had come back to her. That woman Sitara had something other women lacked. Asif left his wife because she probably did not have the qualities that he had found in Sitara. Was it that she had left Asif with no taste for inexperienced virgins?

I have written this account and I know that it will not annoy

Asif because he is a big-hearted man. Sitara, of course, would be angry, but after some time, she will forgive me because, in her own way, she too is a big-hearted woman. In my book, she walks tall. I do not know what she thinks of me but I have always thought of her as a woman who is born once in a hundred years.

NAWAB KAASHMIRI: AN ACTOR'S ACTOR

Though he was merely an actor—I say 'merely' because actors, like writers, are given little respect in this society—I had more respect for him than I have for anyone else who may fall in the 'merely' category. He was a master of his art. This is something about which a cabinet minister may not have been able to tell you anything. But if you had put the same question to a working man in rags who had spent his hard-earned money to see Nawab Kaashmiri in a movie, he would have told you about Nawab's great achievements as an artist. When an English king dies, they announce: 'The King is dead; long live the King.' Nawab Kaashmiri is dead, but there is no one who can take his place and for whose long life I can pray because, compared to him, all actors look like ordinary pawns.

I first met Nawab Kaashmiri in a Bombay studio. We sat together for a long time and talked. I narrated one of my film stories to him but it had no effect on him. He told me without any ceremony, 'It's all right, but I don't like it.' I was impressed by his frank criticism. The next day, I narrated another story of mine to him. At many points in the narrative, I saw tears well up in his eyes. When I was finished, he pulled out a handkerchief, dried his eyes and said, 'Whom are you selling this story to? I would very much like the role of the pimp.' I told him that no producer was prepared to buy the story. 'Let them go to hell,' Nawab said.

I saw him for the first time in *Yahudi ki Ladki*. Rattan Bai was the female lead and Nawab played the Jew traitor. I had never met a Jew in my life, but when I went to Bombay and saw them, I felt that Nawab's rendition had been close to life. He told me that in order to do justice to the part and get it right, he had spent a good deal of time with Bombay's Jews. Only when he was confident that he understood them had he said yes to B.N. Sarkar, owner of New Theatre. He was unforgettable in that movie. He had had all his teeth extracted to lend credibility to his role as an old man. He was indeed a great actor and would never accept a role unless he sincerely felt that he could do justice to it. Before signing a contract, he would listen to the entire story and think about it for several days. He would stand in front of a mirror to get right the various facial expressions the character would need. When he was fully satisfied that he was on top of the character he had been asked to play he would sign the papers.

He loved the plays of Agha Hashra Kashmiri, but it is strange that a man who was one of the most admired actors of the old Imperial Theatrical Company which staged Hashra's major works would so completely change his style after coming to motion pictures. There was no theatricality in his acting style on the screen. He would speak his lines as people talk in daily life. Nawab's performances in Imperial Theatrical Company plays such as *Khoobsoorat Balaa*, *Noor-i-Watan* and *Baagh-i-Iran* made him famous all over the country. He was the only son of the Mufti-i-Azam of the biggest imambara in Lucknow. It is ironical that the son of the Shi'as' biggest religious personality in Lucknow should have gone to the stage and then the cinema, but he had been inclined that way from childhood. The story is that a roving theatrical company once came to Lucknow and the young Nawab used to go and watch its presentations regularly and avidly. He felt that if there was one reason he had come into this world, it was to be an actor. He would come home from the theatre and for hours he would rehearse and repeat the lines of dialogue he had heard earlier that evening.

One day, he appeared at the roving theatrical company and asked that he be tested. When the director saw him act and deliver his lines, he was swept off his feet. Nawab was hired immediately—at what salary, I do not know. He went with the company to Calcutta and established himself there in a very short time. When Cowasji Khataoji of Alfred Theatre Company watched Nawab perform, he made him an offer which he accepted. Before long, he had established his reputation as a character actor. The owner of another famous company, Seth Sukh Lal Karnani, was a colourful character. When he heard that an actor by the name of Nawab was drawing in the audience, he said in his typical style, 'So get hold of that bull.' That bull was got hold of, given a higher salary and for two years he played in every major company production. I am not sure if it was around the time when Bombay's Imperial Film Company was making its first talkie, *Alam Ara*.

The talkies were now here to stay. One of the first men to seize the opportunity was B.N. Sarkar, an educated man of vision, who set up New Theatre and persuaded Nawab to move from the stage to the cinema. He was an admirer of the actor and treated him not as an employee but as one of his heroes. He was a man of literary and artistic taste. Nawab's first film was the celebrated *Yahudi ki Ladki*. The heroine was Rattan Bai, whose hair was so long that it touched her ankles. The movie was directed by the Bengali director Atorthy. The music was scored by Bali. The third member of the team was a man called Hafizji. It was quite a trinity. Atorthy was an educated man. He once said to me, 'An actor like Nawab the world will not see again. He takes to his role as a glove takes to the wearer's hand. He is a master of his art.' Hafizji too used to say that he had never seen an actor like Nawab.

Nawab was offered the role of a pickpocket in a movie by the name of *Maya*. When he heard the story, he refused to take it, saying he could not play it since he was not a pickpocket and did not know how to pick someone's pocket. However, he began spending his time in a third-class Calcutta hangout where he got to know a number of pickpockets and other street characters. He would sit with them and drink, although he was not a drinking man. After a week of this, he was satisfied that he could play the role. He had learnt their ways and become familiar with their tricks. He was a success in the part. In real life, he was a good and pious man. One of his relatives, M.A. Ammad, told me once that he was an observing Shi'a and would never undertake anything major unless he had first prayed and asked for divine guidance. Personally, I do not know the difference between the Sunni and the Shi'a sects. But I do know that when they fight each other, they prove conclusively that they are off their rockers.

Who can forget that scene in the film *Mukti* when Nawab offers his wife, who has been unfaithful to him, a plate of roasted corn. He was able to express more emotion by the mere movement of the hand that held the plate than other actors could with their faces. In *Devdas*, when K.L. Saigal slaps him, he rubs his cheek for a long time, then says, 'You hit Deeno Bhai.' That one line used to run like a strong electric current through the audience. In the movie *Ziddi*, when his nephew's wife, played by Kuldip Kaur, rushes past him—he is in his invalid's chair—with her lover, played by Pran, he looks at her and says philosophically, '*Phur* . . . she is gone.'

As for his personal life, his first wife was from his hometown, but when they had got married, I do not know. There were no children. When he lost hope of her bearing a child, he began to look around and obtained the hand of the daughter of Prince Mehr Qadar, the eldest son of the Nawab of Oudh. When his wife learnt that he had married another woman, she had a breakdown, but Nawab paid no attention. In the end, she committed suicide. She sprinkled kerosene on her quilt, rubbed her body and her clothes with it liberally, calmly lay down on her bed, lit a match and set everything on fire. Nawab was with his new wife in another house, ignorant of how his first wife had greeted the news of his second marriage. When he did learn, he arranged for her burial. She had left a will that said that her life insurance, which was worth ten thousand rupees, should be given to her husband. She had also left him a huge quantity of gold. Nawab was surprised by her last testament. For a long time, he must have smelt kerosene after he was told of it.

When I think of Nawab Kaashmiri, I sometimes feel like a kerosene can, which is about to ignite. I am also a Kashmiri but I am not so cruel as to drive my wife to kill herself just because she could not beget a child. I love Kashmiris but I hate those who ill-treat their wives. I admired Nawab Kaashmiri and I considered him a great artist but whenever I see him on the screen, I smell kerosene.

May God keep him in hell where he would be happier.

Shahida was a happy housewife, married to Mohsin Abdullah. They had fallen in love in Aligarh and married and remained in love. She was the kind of young woman who did not even look at another man, but Mohsin was different. He relished variety, not that Shahida knew anything about it. She did know, though, that her husband's sisters were liberal women and mixed with men without any self-consciousness and even discussed such things as sex with them. Shahida was never comfortable with that. One of Mohsin's sisters, Dr Rashid Jahan, was particularly 'advanced'. She later married Sahibzada Mahmood-ul-Zafar who was teaching at MAO College, Amritsar, where I was a student. He was a handsome man and he had socialist ideas. Faiz Ahmed Faiz, the poet, with whom I had the friendliest of relations, also used to teach at our college and he always reminded me of a lotus-eater. He would often ask me to shop for him, something I would do happily. He used to go to Dehra Dun to meet Dr Rashid Jahan with whom he was in love, I think. I have no idea to what extent he was successful, but I do know that he wrote some wonderful love poems at the time, despite his laziness. I mention these interconnected facts because they form the background to the story I am about to tell.

Mohsin Abdullah moved to Bombay when he landed a job at Bombay Talkies, which was the most prestigious institution of its time, headed by the formidable Himanshu Rai who believed in hiring educated young people. Mohsin worked in the laboratory and lived in the Malad area where the studio was located. It was company policy that middle-level and junior employees live as close to work as possible, and accordingly Mohsin and Shahida had rented an old, dilapidated house in the area. He was a good worker and had made a fine impression on Himanshu Rai. He made about the same money as Ashok Kumar who was fast becoming successful. Azuri, the dancer, and Mumtaz were also at Bombay Talkies, as was S. Mukherjee who was assistant to the sound recordist Savak Vacha. It was a happy crowd.

When *Puner Milan* was being shot—it starred Snehprabha Pradhan, who was an educated girl—Khwaja Ahmad Abbas, the writer (later to become a famous producer), also happened to be employed in the company's publicity department. Mohsin and Abbas both fell in love with Snehprabha who belonged to Sind and had come to Bombay to do a nursing course, which she had successfully completed. They both wanted her to 'nurse' them but she was a smart woman who played both of them along without letting them get anywhere near her. Mohsin had also developed a passion for gambling and would lose his entire salary on his new pastime, much to the misery of Shahida who had to borrow money from her parents every month. They also had a child who was always sick. One day Shahida said to her husband as gently as she could, 'Mohsin, even if you don't take care of me, at least take care of your child.' This had no effect on him because he was obsessed with Snehprabha Pradhan and gambling.

At the time I was working at Nanoobhai Desai's Hindustan Cinetone. V. Shantaram, who had made one hit after another for Prabhat Film Company, had earlier invited me to come to Poona on a get-acquainted visit and meet a group of writers and journalists who were also to be there. One of those invited was W.Z. Ahmed, who was working with Sadhana Bose, translating dialogue from Bengali into Urdu. We spent two days in Poona, but I did not really get to know him. W.Z. Ahmed always wore a kind of mask that was hard to penetrate. Everything about him, including his smile, struck me as a pose. I did notice though that, like the well-known Jewish director Ernst Lubitsch, he always had a long cigar tucked in his mouth. I next met W.Z. at the actor Ramshakal's place where he was drinking rum. We exchanged cold, formal greetings and I could see that he was by nature reserved, like a tortoise which draws in its head so as not to be seen. 'Why don't you say something?' I asked him. He laughed. 'You have been talking to Ramshakal, is that not enough conversation?' he replied. I did not like his answer, which was more suited to a politician, a breed that I hate. I met him several times in the same house but he hardly ever opened his mouth. He would just sit in a corner, quietly drinking rum with the two of us jabbering away.

Two years later, I heard that W.Z. was setting up a film company. I was surprised that a man who was making his living translating dialogue from Bengali to Urdu could do that. He had decided to call it Shalimar Studio and it was to be based in Poona. The first production was already being aggressively advertised. I noticed that every advertisement was centred on a new actress described as 'the inscrutable Neena'. I could not understand what mystery could be attached to an actress. Once she appeared on the screen, all her mystery would be lost. For nearly two years, he kept selling Neena as 'the mystery lady'. I asked many people who this Neena was but no one knew. Once, when I was working for Baburao Patel, editor of *Filmindia*, I asked him who this Neena was. 'Sala, don't you know? What kind of an editor are you . . . You know that Mohsin Abdullah?' Baburao asked. 'Yes, I have heard of him . . . I even know a little bit about him,' I replied. 'Neena is his wife, understand?' Patel said. 'But I don't understand. His wife's name is Shahida,' I replied. Patel then informed me that Shahida was the sister-in-law—bhabhi—of the actress Renuka Devi whom I had seen in *Bhabhi*, a film that had impressed me. So now we had two bhabhis: Renuka and Shahida alias Neena.

I met W.Z. Ahmed a few more times and came to the conclusion that he was both a careful planner and an adventurer. Like Soviet dictators, he would plan for years before embarking on anything. Then he would sit back and wait for results. I am a man in a hurry, so we were temperamentally incompatible. I talked too much; he was a man of few words. He was very formal whereas I hated formality. When he spoke, he sounded like a recording. I must admit though that whatever he said often had a lot of weight. He spoke many languages: Marathi,

Gujarati, English and Punjabi. A Punjabi, he was the brother of Maulana Salahuddin Ahmed, editor of the literary magazine *Adabi Duniya*. Another brother, Riazuddin Ahmed, was a government officer. Most people would not have known that Salahuddin and W.Z. were brothers, though they certainly had one thing in common: they loved flattery. By the way, the 'W' in the name stood for Waheed. He was married to the daughter of Sir Ghulam Hussain Hidayatullah, who was Governor of Sindh after the establishment of Pakistan. How this match had come to be arranged, I haven't the least idea.

I ran into W.Z. Ahmed the other day at my barber's shop on Hall Road, Lahore, and dragged him home where I told him that I wanted to write a piece on Neena and asked him if I had his permission. His answer was typical, 'I will get back to you in a day or two.' Several days passed but I did not hear from him. A few days later when I ran into him again, I asked, 'How much time do you need?' He was smoking a pipe. He smiled vaguely and his half-bald head shone even more. 'I am busy these days. I need a week,' he said. This conversation took place in the office of the film magazine *Director* owned by Chaudhri Fazle Haq and edited by Shabab Keranwi (who later became a film director). 'That's fine, a week goes by quickly,' I replied.

Two more weeks passed and there was no word from him, so I said to myself that actors and actresses were public property and one did not need permission to write about them. Hence the piece that you are now reading.

When Shalimar was established, Mohsin Abdullah was put in charge of the laboratory. Shahida was the domestic type and had no ambition to become a film star; she only wanted a calm home life. W.Z. Ahmed, being the Soviet-style planner that he was, drew up a five-year plan and began to implement it stage by stage. He aroused no suspicion, using his tortoise technique. Mohsin, meanwhile, was busy trying to entice Snehprabha Pradhan. He was also very hard up, had given his gambling losses, so one day he said to Shahida, 'You are so conservative. Look at my sisters; how modern and enlightened they are.' She replied that she was quite happy the way she was. There were many arguments between the two because Mohsin wanted her to become an actress, a line of work in which she had no interest.

Ismat Chughtai, the writer and wife of director-writer Shahid Latif who was associated with such famous films as *Ziddi*, *Arzoo* and *Buzdil*, told my wife, Safia, that Shahida and she had been at school in Aligarh and she knew what a simple girl she was. 'How do you know?' my wife asked. 'I know, she is my friend,' Ismat replied. 'What do you think of me?' my wife asked. 'You are just a woman,' Ismat answered. 'Is there something wrong with that?' my wife asked. 'No, but you are different from Shahida,' replied Ismat. 'How?' 'She is artless, you are not. You know how to keep an eye on your husband; she does not.' 'Tell me more.' 'I know her well. I know her whole family. She was really a very simple girl. We used to make fun of her in college.' Ismat told my wife that Shahida knew nothing about men or falling in love and she for one could not understand how she had fallen in love with Mohsin and married him. He must have chased her hard and she must have relented because she had a soft personality. Naive by nature, she could never work out the consequences of the actions that she took.

In the end, Mohsin succeeded in persuading his wife to join the movies though it was against her instincts. Shalimar Studio, therefore, was built on her fragile shoulders. Ahmed became a producer and turned the simple Shahida into 'Neena, the mystery girl'. He ran a huge publicity campaign to introduce his star. You only had to pick up a movie magazine in those days to read about her. This propaganda barrage created much public curiosity because people were keen to know who this mysterious star was. The film that launched her career was *Ek Raat*, based on Hardy's *Tess*. Shahida had been given the role of the peasant girl who is raped and then married off. She is so simple that she tells the story to her husband who throws her out.

Ahmed's five-year plan was on course. He would meet Shahida as Molotov would meet an ambassador. Mohsin was doing his own thing, though he was not having much luck with Snehprabha. Ahmed had become a close friend of Shahida's and would call her 'Begum' and treat her with great deference. He would rise when she entered the room, bowing from the waist to greet her. This was all well thought out. He wanted her to notice the difference between him and the unconcerned Mohsin. He was prepared to wait, one, two, even five years. He knew that ultimately he would capture her. In moviedom, most men succeed through women. Ahmed knew that and so he kept Mohsin happy while keeping an eye on his wife. He had hired Mohsin on a good salary so that he would get even more involved in his favourite pastimes. Shahida would complain to Mohsin off and on about his conduct, but it had no effect on him. From the confining atmosphere of Bombay Talkies, he had been catapulted into the open spaces of Shalimar and he was taking full advantage of this freedom. Shahida may have become an actress but she still wanted to return to private life. She did not much like being called 'the mystery girl'.

But as time passed and she began to excite people's curiosity, she began to change. She became sensitive to the differences between Ahmed and Mohsin. While one was the very picture of good manners and thoughtfulness, the other was rude and careless. Shahida's biggest embarrassment was the unabashed manner in which Mohsin chased women. Ahmed had put Mohsin in charge of the laboratory but he knew that he would not be able to manage it. It was all part of his plan. He had never asked Mohsin why he gambled or went to the races or ran after studio girls. He wanted him to get even more involved in these diversions. It was all very obvious but not to the simple Shahida. She did not even realize that she herself was changing. She would sit in front of the mirror while make-up was being applied, look at herself and blush. She sometimes felt like Tess who was going to be raped. When shooting began, she became less self-conscious. There was now a widening gulf between Mohsin and her, something she did not want, but Ahmed kept assuring her that there was no cause for worry because the relationship would heal by itself. Ahmed moved slowly and with care, finally convincing Shahida with the greatest subtlety that her husband was dissolute and a wastrel. He also made her realize that he had given him a job because of his concern for him but he had to confess that Mohsin had betrayed his trust.

This was indeed true. Mohsin's work at the laboratory was not satisfactory, and though Ahmed had an abundance of patience, one day he sent for Mohsin Abdullah and said to him in his soft voice, 'Perhaps you do not do what needs to be done because you think this sort of work is beneath you. I am prepared to continue paying you your salary, but I am going to place the laboratory under someone else's charge.' Mohsin's first reaction was anger, but Ahmed cooled him down and put him on the promised pension which, for all practical purposes, it was. Mohsin, who could be either highly sensitive or utterly otherwise, must have been feeling 'otherwise' when he accepted Ahmed's offer. He also seemed to be oblivious of the fact that his long-neglected wife, whom he always wanted to see emulating his 'enlightened' sisters, was slowly being drawn to another man. The fact was that he was not really much interested in his wife, preferring his horse races in Poona and Bombay and his card-playing to her.

Meanwhile, the film was progressing and Ahmed, being the director, was using every opportunity his position gave him to wean Shahida away from her husband, who had failed to realize that his virtual dissociation from the studio could affect his relationship with his wife. He was foolishly confident that since theirs had been a love marriage she would always remain faithful to him. Ahmed was a man who kept his word and he was paying Mohsin his salary in time even when there was not enough money to pay others. Not by nature mean or small-minded, he exhibited all the qualities generally associated with people who come from good families and solid backgrounds. He was in the movie business, although by temperament he was more suited to politics. He had brought no capital with him but had enough tact and imagination to raise millions. He never wasted his money on frivolities, but he had one weakness. He would hold court like a Mughal prince and lap up the flattery heaped on him by his hangers-on.

Ahmed had a whole stable of writers and poets working for him, among them Sagar Nizami, Josh Malihabadi, Jan Nisar Akhtar, Krishan Chander and Bharat Vyas, apart from Dr Abdullah Chughtai and my nephew Masood Pervez. They would sit in Ahmed's room and hold heated discussions on the film being shot, sometimes for the whole night, but without arriving at any useful conclusions, which was not surprising as the atmosphere was that of a court full of sycophants. Josh would be kept happy with a pint of rum every evening. He would come up with a verse that was appropriate to the subject under discussion and receive effusive praise. Masood Pervez, who was very quick-minded in those days, would add a few verses on the spot, which would inspire Sagar Nizami, who would recite an entire poem in his sweet voice. Krishan Chander, being a story writer, would just sit there like an owl, unable to join in the spontaneous versification. Very little work would get done during such meetings. Bharat Vyas would feel out of it because of his poor knowledge of Urdu. To make up, he would try to impress the company with his Sanskritized Hindi. And every time Ahmed said something witty, Josh would shower him with praise, 'Ahmed sahib, you are a poet.' When the meeting came to an end, Ahmed would shut himself in his room and try to write a ghazal, but as far as I know, he had not been able to compose one even once. All these people were Ahmed's groupies.

In the beginning, everyone used to be paid regularly but it did not last. The permanent staff had to subsist on advances. The atmosphere at Shalimar was strange. There was one director with about a dozen assistants, who, I suspect, had their own assistants. How these people managed to survive, I never could understand. It was a tribute to Ahmed that he had somehow kept Shalimar going because he was a clever man who remained cool no matter how hard the times were. He would just sit there unperturbed, pick out a betel leaf from a silver paandaan, add his favourite condiments, including a pinch of tobacco, roll the leaf, place it in his mouth, and smile.

He had every quality that a successful politician needs, and that was how he had been able to set up Shalimar Studio. That was also how he had stolen Shahida from her husband. I could never understand what was so attractive about her that he had built an entire studio practically on her body. Could it be that she was the only woman he could get? The fact was that she was not the acting type at all, so what was it about her that he had found so irresistible? Was he so impressed with her housewifely qualities that he had fallen in love with her? It is also possible that he was not in love with her at all, but had simply used her for his own purposes. And although he had worked long and hard to wrest her away from Mohsin, I do not think he ever succeeded fully because even when Mohsin and she were going through a divorce Shahida did not want to leave him. But in the end, she really did leave him; she lived alone for a while and ultimately moved in with Ahmed.

Which year it was I no longer remember, but I was working at Filmistan with S. Mukherjee as the company's production controller. One day he asked me why I did not write a story for him. I sat down and turned out four stories in five days, but when he asked me to read them to him, I refused and sent all four to my nephew Masood Pervez who worked for Ahmed at Shalimar, as I have stated earlier. The first story was called 'Controlistan'. Four days later, I travelled to Poona. The first thing that I did on arrival at Shalimar was to go to the loo because it is my view that if you wanted to know quickly what was going on all you had to do was read the graffiti. 'Nobody gets paid here; the rest is OK,' was the first news that greeted me. That was enough to nearly make me take the next train back to Bombay but Masood insisted that I meet Ahmed now that I was here. We met in his office. He was in his chair, a long cigar between his lips. On one side sat Shahida, on the other Josh Malihabadi, with whom I exchanged greetings. He was holding a pint of rum, courtesy, no doubt, W.Z. Ahmed. I spoke to Ahmed in Punjabi but immediately realized that Shahida and Josh did not understand the language, so I slipped into Urdu. When I had first seen Ahmed at Prabhat he was a fine, handsome young man but he now looked somewhat burnt out. He greeted me with his usual courtesy and introduced me to Shahida alias Neena the mystery girl. She was plain and there was no mystery to her whatever. She looked like a watercolour that has been under a dripping tap and as a result taken on an even more washed-out look. There was nothing actress-like about her. She just sat there in her chair quietly. She knew who I was and she also must have known that Mohsin was a friend of mine. I mostly talked to Josh, who was holding on tightly to his daily ration of rum, while Ahmed was mimicking one of Bombay's German film directors. We never talked about the story which I had come to sell. I had a couple of drinks, and when I have had a couple, I do not stand on ceremony. So I turned towards Neena and told her, 'I do not know where your mystery lies, but I do know that you cheated your husband.' Ahmed looked at me, apologized that he would have to step out for a minute because he had to see someone and, before leaving, he took Josh with him. He had stolen Shahida under a long-term scheme as one steals a pigeon from a pigeon coop. So now that he had her, he wanted her to lay any eggs that she might wish to lay in his coop. It was not Neena who was mysterious but Ahmed. She had laid an egg at Mohsin's, which had not produced a very healthy chick, but Ahmed was taking as good care of it as if he were the mother.

After Ahmed and Josh left, I had a conversation with Neena, telling her that Mohsin often pined for her. An ironic smile appeared on her wilted lips and she said, 'Manto sahib, you do not know that man. Every tear that he sheds is a crocodile tear. It is not he who sheds tears but tears which shed him.' I did not know what that meant but the grimness with which she spoke suggested that she was convinced that whatever she had said was true.

Ahmed in the meanwhile had begun making preparations to film *Meerabai*. He had chosen Bharat Bhushan to play Krishna, but since he was very thin, he used to be fed lumps of butter and other nourishing food every day so that he would put on weight and look the part. It was yet another five-year Ahmed plan.

Let me also tell the story of Ahmed's first and real wife, Safia, daughter of Sir Ghulam Hussain Hidayatullah. When a man neglects his wife, she is bound to go with another, which was what happened in this case. It is said that Safia began an affair with the famous communist leader Syed Sibt-e-Hassan. Years later, I asked Sibt-e-Hassan in Lahore about it and wanted to know if it was true that he had followed Safia to America where she had gone to some conference and, further, that the two of them had got married. Had Sibt-e-Hassan not been arrested by the government soon after our conversation, I would have solved the mystery. He was released after three years and when I met him soon afterwards there were too many people around for me to bring it up. 'When will you go to jail again?' I asked instead. He drew at his pipe and replied, 'In a few days.' Just as he had said, fifteen days later, he was in jail again.

But let me get back to our story. It was I who helped Mohsin Abdullah get a job at Filmistan because he was in a bad way. I told S. Mukherjee, 'Are you not ashamed that Mohsin and you were once colleagues at Bombay Talkies and while you are the big boss at Filmistan, the production controller of the company, your old friend is almost starving?' Mukherjee sent for him the next day and hired him at Rs 400 a month, regardless of the fact that Mohsin never did much work, expecting others to do it for him. We were very busy with *Eight Days*, a film I had written, and Mohsin would keep advising me about the script, something I would ignore because it was always technically absurd. He would also tell me that he still missed Shahida, though I knew he was trying to start an affair with Veera, a young woman we had picked up for a starring role in *Eight Days*. Mohsin normally used to travel second class on the train that brought us every morning to Filmistan, a trip of about twenty miles from Bombay, but after Veera was hired by Rai Bahadur Chunilal, Mohsin would travel only first class, just to impress her.

One day I was in a taxi going down Lamington Road when I spied Mohsin. I told the driver to stop. 'Mohsin, what's up?' I asked. A smile appeared on his broad face. 'These days I measure the roads with my feet,' he replied. 'How long and broad is Lamington Road then?' I asked. 'As long as you and as broad as me,' he answered. 'Get into the taxi and I will drop you wherever you have to go,' I offered, but he did not accept my invitation. He looked restless and I could understand why. He had lost his wife to Ahmed (the two were living together in Poona) and Snehprabha Pradhan was paying no attention to him. He had lost whatever money he had in gambling, and to top it all he had no work. 'And how is Miss Pradhan?' I asked. He smiled bitterly. 'She is all right. Khwaja Ahmad Abbas is trying his luck with her these days. I predict he will lose all his hair in two to three months.' 'Why?' I asked. 'You do not know her. She is not a woman, she is a safety razor and what she shaves off never grows again.' I have always had a lot of body hair and I wished for a moment I could get hold of this miracle safety razor called Miss Pradhan so as to be rid of all that ungainly hair. Luckily, I did not try or I would have met the same fate as Khwaja Ahmad Abbas and Mohsin Abdullah. Both of them eventually went bald.

BABURAO PATEL: THE SOFT-HEARTED
ICONOCLAST

I think it was in 1938 that I first met Baburao Patel. I was at the time editing the weekly *Mussawar* on a monthly salary of forty rupees. Nazir Ludhianwi, who owned the magazine, was keen that I make some extra money, which was why he had introduced me to Baburao Patel, the editor of *Filmindia*.

Before I write about that meeting, let me first say a few words about how *Filmindia* came to be born. There was a time when the Poona-based Prabhat Film Company was at the height of its success, having already produced such runaway all-India hits as *Amrit Manthan* and *Amar Jyoti*. It was no longer just another company but a nationally acclaimed institution. Everyone who worked for it exuded the confidence and self-assurance that had become the company's hallmark. On its rolls were men like V. Shantaram, Saeed Fatelal and K. Dhailbar, who tried to excel their rivals in the art and technique of film-making. As a result, the company had grown in strength and reputation, and had already given birth to three siblings: Famous Pictures, the sole distribution agency for Prabhat movies, headed by Baburao Pai; B.B. Samant and Company, in charge of the printing and production of the entire range of Prabhat publicity materials; and the New Jack Printing Press, which, though unknown in the trade, was entrusted with the actual job of printing all posters, handbills and books relating to Prabhat movies. It was headed by a man named Parker.

Filmindia was a child of the New Jack Printing Press as Parker and Baburao Patel were good friends. Parker did not have much of an education but the plan to launch a magazine was as much his as his friend's. They had the press and paper, was easily available because it was cheap in those days. B.B. Samant and Company could be depended upon to provide the advertising, not only for Prabhat-made movies but possibly others as well. All essential ingredients were in place. Baburao was a hard-working and thorough man who did not believe in dreaming, and as the English idiom has it, he liked to hit the nail on the head. It is a fact that with its very first issue *Filmindia* started a new trend in Indian film journalism.

Baburao wrote with eloquence and power. He had a sharp and inimitable sense of humour, often hurtful. There was a tough-guy assertiveness about his writing. He could also be venomous in a way that no other writer of English in India has ever been able to match. What established his name and reputation was his subtle sense of satire, mixed with aggressiveness, which had been until then unknown in Indian journalistic writing. Soon he had his readers hooked on his stuff.

He was a man of great dignity. You realized it the moment you set foot in the large office he had set up in Mubarak Building on Bombay's Apollo Street. That was where I first met him. By then, about seven or eight issues of *Filmindia* had appeared, which one simply could not fail to admire. I had imagined that the author of such elegant and finely honed humour would be slim and good-looking, but when I saw a peasant sitting in a revolving chair behind a huge table, I was disappointed. There was nothing in his features to even remotely connect him with his writing. He had small eyes embedded in a big face and his nose was large and bulbous. His teeth were not very good and he had a big forehead. When he rose to shake hands with me, I realized that he was much taller than I was and quite a strong man. His handshake, however, was limp. For me the caving in of the roof, so to speak, came when he began to talk in Urdu. He was a peasant and, like all true Bombaywalas, every sentence that came out of his mouth was liberally studded with the word 'sala'. He also had a wide vocabulary of swear words.

I first thought that he spoke like that because his grip on Urdu was weak, but when he got on the phone I became convinced that this man could never be the Baburao Patel who wrote those delightful *Filmindia* editorials or the 'Bombay Calling' column, or who came up with those amusing answers to questions sent to the magazine. His accent was atrocious; he sounded as if he was speaking English in Marathi and Marathi in street Bombayese. And, of course, before every full stop, there was the ubiquitous 'sala'. So I said to myself, 'If this sala is Baburao Patel then this sala, that is me, is not Saadat Hasan Manto.' Nazir Ludhianwi, who had introduced me to Patel, praised me effusively. 'I know,' said Patel, 'that sala Abid Gulrez often comes here and reads *Mussawar* to me every week.' Then he turned to me. 'And what does this sala name Manto mean?' I calmly explained to him what it meant. He then asked me if I would translate a Prabhat film booklet—'chopri' in Gujarati—into Urdu. I took the booklet that Baburao Patel had written, translated it and asked Nazir Ludhianwi to pass it on to Baburao. I was told that he liked it very much.

We did not meet for a while as most of my time was spent at the *Mussawar* office, and because even in those days I considered it undignified to run after film companies in search of work. I learnt, though, that Baburao had talked V. Shantaram into bringing out a magazine called *Prabhat*, which would publicize, but in an original way, the production of this thriving film company. Shantaram may have been a man of limited education but he had the temperament of an artist who always wished to break new ground. He readily agreed and Baburao brought out the magazine, which delivered exactly what he had promised. It was well produced and it was original. It certainly did a great public relations job for Prabhat Film Company. Nazir Ludhianwi was the kind of person who never let a good opportunity pass, so one day he suggested to Baburao that some sections of his new magazine should be reproduced in *Mussawar* in Urdu translation. Baburao agreed because he had once known poverty and he always had a soft corner for those who needed work. He knew all about Nazir's precarious financial situation, and when he learnt that I would be doing the translations he felt reassured and gave him the go-ahead.

To tell the truth, my knowledge of English was limited. What

Baburao wrote, though not beyond my ken, was not easy to translate with precision either. He had a certain style and his use of language was different from that of others. He was familiar with both English and American usage and he had a natural talent for playing with words. I decided that the best way to translate him was to read what he had written and put it in my own words, taking care to retain the spirit of the original. When Nazir took the first issue to Baburao, I was with him. He looked at me and said, 'Sala, are you trying to be Baburao?' His cigarette was nestling, villager style, between the third and the little fingers of his right hand and he drew on it vigorously. 'Yesterday, I sala had this stuff read to me by Abid Gulrez. I enjoyed it . . . then I said to him (here he swore) "Hey you! Weren't you saying that this sala is a big-time Urdu writer?"' I accepted the compliment because it was one. It was decided that the arrangement would continue. Unfortunately, the magazine folded after two issues because Prabhat felt it could not afford the expense.

I will not go into details about the magazine because they will draw me into areas I do not wish to be drawn into. What I really want is to write about Baburao Patel and my impressions of him. Because of certain things, my relation with Nazir . . . no, no, no, that comes later . . . Well, it happened that I decided to get married. I left the magazine and got a job with Imperial Film Company at eighty rupees a month, but it only lasted a year, with Imperial owing me four months' salary. My next job was with Saroj Film Company. I had just joined when rumours began to circulate that the company was going to sink. Was I jinxed? The company did go bust but thanks to some quick footwork, our boss, Seth Nanoobhai Desai, managed to set up another company on the debris of the defunct Saroj and I was hired at a hundred rupees a month. Three-fourths of a story that I had written had already been filmed. In the meantime, my nikah had also taken place and all that remained was for me to bring my bride home. But I needed money to rent a flat where we could live. So what was I to do but go see Seth Nanoobhai and ask him for some cash which he flatly refused to part with. I told him of my situation but it had no effect on him. We got into

an argument and he fired me. That was a shattering blow. I felt
so insulted that I decided to stage a hunger strike bang in front
of the company. Someone must have told Baburao because he
picked up the phone and abused Seth Nanoobhai and when that
had no effect he arrived in person and, after a long discussion,
persuaded him to settle my dues in part, if not in full. Though
I was owed twelve hundred rupees, I was paid eight hundred
rupees, which I pocketed on the basis of the old maxim that
something is better than nothing. It did enable me though to
bring my wife home.

I forgot to mention that during my time at Imperial, one of the
actresses with the company, the quiet and modest Padma Devi,
who played the lead in my first film *Kisan Kanya*, which was in
colour, had a thing going with Baburao Patel. He used to keep
a stern eye on her. He already had two wives, one of whom, a
doctor, I had once seen.

Meanwhile, Nazir Ludhianwi had behaved badly with me and
terminated my services. My sincere and selfless friendship and all
the hard work I had done for him had been disregarded. Besides
a salary, he used to pay me a monthly house rent allowance of
twenty-five rupees, which I now lost, but I was not sorry. I was
doing some radio writing but more money was needed because
I had a family now. My old mother was also living with me. To
celebrate my wedding, I had thrown a party for my friends from
the film industry, but it was clear that my mother would not be
able to manage the party chores on her own. I was in a bit of a
fix when something unexpected happened. Somehow, Baburao
came to find out and the next thing I knew Padma Devi had
arrived at my flat and was helping my mother with the cooking.
She had also brought some sort of an ornament for my wife as
a wedding gift.

I went to see Baburao after some days. I knew that just to
help his friend Abid Gulrez he had brought out the Urdu weekly
Karwan, but Abid, a poet, was the carefree kind, and had left
to try his luck in the movies, writing dialogue, film scripts and
lyrics. I showed Baburao the dismissal letter Nazir had sent me.
He was taken aback, but he recovered, abused everyone and

asked, 'So?' I knew he was about to offer me a job, so I nodded my head to indicate that I would say yes. Baburao spoke again, 'Sala, why don't you come here? There is this sala magazine *Karwan* with nobody to look after it.'

'I am ready,' I answered.

Baburao shouted, 'Rita!'

The door opened and a strong-legged, bosomy, dark-complexioned Christian girl walked into the room. Baburao winked at her. 'Come here.' She walked up to his chair. 'Turn around,' Baburao told her. When she did, he slapped her bottom resoundingly. 'Get some paper and a pencil.' The girl who was called Rita Carlyle was Baburao's secretary, stenographer and mistress, all in one. When she returned with a shorthand notebook and a pencil, Baburao started dictating my appointment letter to her. When he came to my salary, he stopped. 'Well Manto, what will it be?'

Then without waiting for a reply, he said, 'A hundred and fifty will do.'

'No,' I said.

Baburao became serious. 'Look Manto . . . This sala magazine *Karwan* cannot afford more.'

'You got me wrong,' I told him. 'I will work for sixty rupees a month, neither more nor less.'

Baburao thought I was joking, but when I assured him that I was serious, he said in his characteristically peasant way, 'Sala mad mullah!'

I replied, 'Mad mullah I may be, but I have asked for sixty rupees because I will come and go when I want. *Karwan*, I can assure you, will continue to appear on time.'

We agreed that we had a deal.

I worked with Baburao for six or seven months and, during this time, I came to know a lot about his strange personality. He was in love with Rita Carlyle and it was his opinion that no woman in the world could excel her in beauty and charm. Rita Carlyle was not a one-man woman but because of Baburao she had become more upmarket. I am sure if only she could speak Urdu, he would have made her a top film star in a short time. He believed that if he were to pick up a piece of wood and declare it to be the world's greatest dancer, after some time it would indeed become one and the world would acknowledge it too. Padma Devi was not well known when he took charge of her, but he transformed her into the film industry's 'Colour Queen'. He used to print dozens of her pictures in *Filmindia* with witty captions, which he used to write himself.

He was a self-made man. Whatever he was then and whatever he became later was entirely due to his own efforts. He owed nothing to anybody. In his early youth, he had fallen out with his father and cut off all relations with him. Whenever I asked him about Patel the elder, he would invariably say, 'That sala is a pucca bastard.' While it is difficult for me to say which of the two was a pucca bastard, I can say that if the elder Patel was one, then Baburao was a much bigger one.

An analysis of his pungent style would take us back to his childhood. Baburao was always bringing people down from their high pedestals and demolishing shibboleths. Was it because when he was young his father had tried to tame him so that he would become like him? He had also forced him to marry against his will. The second marriage was Baburao's own doing, but this time it was he who had made a mistake. In his pantheon, there were scores of half-shattered statues of the great and the famous—all lying on their faces—scores of old, senile bastards, and hundreds of courtesans and prostitutes. He had demolished them all, deriving the same pleasure in this act as Mahmud of Ghazni must have experienced when despoiling the great temple at Somnath.

Baburao simply could not stand anyone who put on airs. On the other hand, he was always willing to walk a mile to pick up someone who had fallen by the wayside and make him stand upright again. But, once he had him standing, he did everything in his power to bring him down. He was a bundle of contradictions. There was a time when he considered V. Shantaram the world's greatest film director, but when he turned against him he tried to demolish not only his movies but also the man himself. He used to hate the director-producer A.R. Kardar but when he became his friend Kardar could do no wrong. Then came 1947 and he denounced Kardar and tried his best to have his studio and his property confiscated by the government on the ground that the owner had gone to Pakistan and abandoned his assets. Kardar was lucky and survived the assault.

Once Baburao had announced that it was only the 'Mian Bhais'—a nickname for Muslims—who knew how to make movies because no Hindu was capable of equalling the style, methodology, technique and artistry, which were natural to Muslim directors. I remember the days when he considered Prithviraj of no more significance than a crawling insect. He also used to feel the same way towards Kishore Sahu. These extreme likes and dislikes were like fits that would periodically affect him. Psychologically, he was unbalanced; some blind and powerful force always kept ramming his insides. It was my view that he was an artist who was so supremely confident of his own talent that he had lost his way. When I was working for *Karwan*, you could not make him stop praising me but when I left he would say to people if my name came up, 'Manto . . . who is that monster?' But Baburao being Baburao, when my film *Eight Days* was released, he wrote that Manto was India's most brilliant, most extraordinary storyteller.

During Baburao's association with Prabhat Film Company, Shanta Apte was considered India's most glamorous film actress, but the moment she left the outfit she became the ugliest woman in India. Baburao wrote such venomous pieces about her in *Filmindia* that, being the true Maharashtrian that she was, she burst into Baburao's office one day, dressed in her riding gear, and whipped him six or seven times with her riding crop. Years earlier, the grand old man of Bombay's English journalism, B.G. Horniman, had taken a few swipes at Baburao in *Bombay Sentinel*. This had angered Baburao so much that he had filed a defamation suit against him, much to the amusement of the eighty-year-old editor who sent a message to him through a common friend that if he did not want his nose bloodied, he should quietly slip him two thousand rupees and the entire episode would be forgotten. Baburao's first reaction had been anger; but on reflection he had sent Horniman a thousand rupees and called it quits.

Baburao may have been foolish and at times frivolous but he was very human with a soft corner for the poor. At that time, postmen were not allowed to use lifts when delivering mail to high-rise buildings but were required to take the stairs. Baburao wrote so much on this inhuman practice that it was finally discontinued. His services to Indian cinema are too numerous to list. Western film-makers who used to make fun of Indian movies and India itself had met their match in Baburao, who gave them a run for their money. He toured Europe, met many of Indian cinema's detractors and gave them his frank views about the quality of the stuff they inflicted on the world.

Baburao must have fathered many children; if not dozens, certainly a dozen. One day when I went to his house, he told all his brood to appear so that I could see them. He was a most affectionate father, but . . . this 'but' marks the point where I bring out the 'other' Baburao. I noticed it when he was beginning to evolve into his other persona. I felt that the resentment he always bore against authority was beginning to get out of hand. I was afraid it were going to assume horrifying proportions if it were not checked, which was what happened. Irked by the popularity of Jawaharlal Nehru, he denounced him as Gandhi's protégé and a nuisance for the entire nation. After Pakistan's establishment, he turned against the new country because he could see it making a place for itself in the world, which ran counter to his petulant temperament.

Filmindia, as the name suggested, should have had only material related to films but slowly it began to get politicized. Things reached a point where politics, filmdom and sex became so inextricably intertwined in its pages that one could only explain them as being a reflection of Baburao Patel's own perverted personality. You could read in one place, all together, about Pakistan, Morarji Desai, women's menstrual problems and about actress Veera's 'papaya-like face'. He even turned against Gandhiji. Did he think politics was a Rita, a Sushila or a Padma whom he could put like a puppet on a string, have it perform tricks according to his instructions? He was too intelligent a man not to know that he had failed as a film-maker and that his chances of succeeding in politics were even slimmer; or was it that he could not help finding fault with everything, that being his nature!

My own theory is that Baburao was not interested in India or Pakistan; he only hated eminence, including the eminence of age and genius. Otherwise he was quite happy in his expensive Oomer Park bungalow, as he was with his secretary Sushila Rani whom he praised to the sky for two years in *Filmindia*. He even had her star in a film and to save her from the lascivious advances of other men he directed the film himself, with disastrous results. Not that he cared because he had his Rani, his race horses, his luxurious office and his suspected cancer, which he was confident he could deal with any time he chose to fly to America.

There was one and only one thing, however, which constantly gnawed at Baburao's heart. He could neither forget it nor come to terms with it. He could not understand why Muslims were undependable. It was not that some of them had betrayed him; so had many Hindus. He was bitter because he liked them. He felt comfortable with them, the way they lived, even the way they looked. Most of all, he loved their food. He was an enlightened man with an open and secular mind, but when one of his daughters fell in love with a Muslim worker in his press, he was upset. The man was illiterate and the girl, being Baburao's daughter, was well bred and educated, but love is impervious to such things, and the two of them, sensing opposition from the family, ran away. Baburao, who managed to find and bring them back, cursed his daughter and ordered her to end the affair but she refused. 'What do you want?' he finally asked her. 'I want to marry him,' she replied. 'All right then,' he said and set about making arrangements for the marriage. I met him some time later and when he began to talk about it there were tears in his eyes. 'What kind of people are you . . . you sala Mussalman? You snatch away our chhokri and then you ask us for food.'

Baburao's later anti-Muslim writings should perhaps be

analysed in the light of this episode. Can there be anything more foolish than to avenge the wrongs of a few by damning an entire community or a religion? Baburao was a student of history. Did he not know that religion and nationalism are realities and not a mirage in the desert? People can continue to say bad things about Islam and the man who brought its message to the world, but it makes not the least difference. So much hatred was spread against the idea of Pakistan, but it came into being. What is particularly tragic is to see an artist succumbing to hatred and bigotry. It should not be in the nature of an artist to hurt others. Baburao Patel was an artist but he degenerated into an ordinary mortal.

Some of *Filmindia*'s later issues made me sick because I just could not believe Baburao had sunk so low. It seemed that the artist who had once inhabited his soul had either turned into a cancer in his belly or now lay buried in the cut and blow-dried hair of Rita Carlyle or the beds of Padma Devi and Sushila, cursed by his two wives.

Chal Chal Re Naujawan had bombed at the box office, a shock that we at Filmistan were slowly trying to absorb. Meanwhile, Gyan Mukherjee was busy writing a war propaganda story for us. We had signed up the actress Nalini Jaywant, and a Rs 25,000 contract, duly approved by her husband, Virendra Desai, had been finalized. It was valid for a year. However, the story had yet to be passed by the censors, this being wartime. S. Mukherjee took a full ten months before he was satisfied with the story idea and the treatment. He always took time making up his mind. Gyan was sent to Delhi to clear the story with the censors, which he managed without difficulty. However, just as shooting was due to begin, Virendra Desai insisted that another contract be signed with Nalini Jaywant since the earlier one was about to run out. Rai Bahadur Chunilal, our owner, was a tough man in these matters and decided to go to court rather than sign a fresh contract. He lost the case, which placed the studio under a further financial obligation of Rs 25,000.

Rai Bahadur Chunilal was keen that the film should be over and done with quickly because enough time had already gone by, so he sent for the director Wali Sahib and his wife, the dancer and actress Mumtaz Shanti, and signed them up. He slipped them an advance of Rs 14,000 under the table without asking for a receipt so that the studio wouldn't have to show it in its books. On the second day of shooting, everyone agreed that the rushes of a brief exchange between Ashok Kumar, the lead, and Mumtaz Shanti, the heroine, were awful. Mumtaz used to come to the studio wearing a burqa and Wali had made it clear that she was not to be so much as touched, so everything was a bit stilted. This inhibiting deal was unacceptable because there were scenes where she would have to be shown semi-nude. It was inevitable that Mumtaz Shanti would be fired and so she was, and thus another Rs 14,000 went down the drain with her. Because of the failure of *Chal Chal Re Naujawan*, the financial health of the company was poor and it was already in the red to the tune of Rs 39,000 without an inch of film to show for it.

One day, Savak Vacha, Dattaram Pai, Ashok and I were chatting about our troubles when Ashok told us that the Rs 14,000 which Rai Bahadur Chunilal had given to Mumtaz was borrowed from him. He was scratching his knee when he said it and it sounded rather comical. We burst out laughing but stopped as we noticed a rather attractive woman going towards the make-up room. Pai looked lecherously at her and nudged Ashok. 'Who is she?'

Vacha smacked him gently over his head. 'Sala, why do you want to know?' As Pai got up, Vacha pulled at his wrist. 'Sit down, don't bother going after her. One look at you and she will run away in horror.' Pai quietened down but Ashok, who had been silent so far, spoke, 'She is not bad-looking, is she?' 'Not displeasing to the eye,' I suggested. 'What?' Ashok asked, not having understood my Urdu. 'I mean the woman who just went past us is pleasant looking, a bit short though but she will do, won't she, Vacha?' Pai asked. 'Dadamoni, you do know who she is, don't you?' Vacha asked. 'No,' Ashok answered. 'All that Mukherjee told me earlier this morning was that there was to be a screen test today.'

When we saw the rushes and heard the sound of her voice, there were different opinions. Ashok, Vacha and I did not like her because her movements were wooden and she moved her body in an unnatural way. When she spoke she raised her eyebrows like a professional dancing girl. Her smile wasn't very nice either. However, Pai seemed to have developed a crush on her and told Mukherjee, 'She has a wonderful screen face.' In the end, she was chosen for the forthcoming war propaganda film, despite our reservations, but on a low monthly salary. Her name was Paro and she would report to the studio every day. She came from the courtesans' quarter, had a happy disposition and was extremely friendly. She came from Meerut where she was a big hit with all the rich men of the city. She had money of her own and quite a bit of it; all she wanted was to become an actress. When I got to know her a little more, it turned out that among those who frequented her kotha were the poets Josh Malihabadi and Sagar Nizami.

Her pronunciation was excellent and she had a lovely skin. In her half-sleeved tight blouse, her arms looked as if they were made of ivory. Her skin was translucent like freshly shaved wood. She would come early, looking washed, scrubbed and very clean, wearing a white or a light-coloured sari. When she left for home in the evening, she would look just as fresh as she did in the morning. Pai was smitten. We had not yet begun shooting and there was plenty of leisure time. Pai would never miss an opportunity to engage Paro in conversation. How she found him attractive, we could not understand. But then she was a courtesan and courtesans have a lot of patience with every male type.

I was given an outline of the movie story to study and suggest additions and deletions. I found the whole thing so disjointed that I was at a loss and did not know what to propose because it had neither head nor tail. But since I felt as if I were on trial, I knocked it into some sort of shape. I was also keen to do my best because it was to be directed by Savak Vacha, who was a very good friend of mine.

When the new outline was presented before the full bench of Filmistan, I felt as if I were in the dock. S. Mukherjee's verdict was short and quick, 'Good, but there is much room for improvement.' When Gyan Mukherjee was asked, he first kept his mouth shut, then finally emitted just one sentence, 'It's almost all right.' He was the man whose name used to appear as director on all movies directed by S. Mukherjee when he had not directed even a single foot of the film. But that was how we worked at Filmistan. Pai, who had no idea what a film story was, would frequently advise me on how to write one. Only someone who has ever written a propaganda movie can understand how trying the task can be. My difficulty was that I had to write a role for Paro, keeping in mind her looks and the way she talked and carried herself. At last the script was finalized and the work started.

We decided that Paro's scenes would be shot last as, by that time, she would be used to the atmosphere of the studio and may also have lost her fear of the camera. However, scene or no scene, she was always on the set. Pai had become quite friendly with her to the extent that they would play tricks on one another. I found Pai's constant attentions to Paro somewhat annoying and when Paro was not around I would make fun of him. His reaction was always the same. 'Sala, why are you jealous?' Paro was a cheerful girl and she became popular with everyone in the studio. The junior staff began to call her Paro Devi out of respect and the name caught on and was even used in the movie credits. Pai, meanwhile, decided to take things one step further and arrived at her house one day where he was offered much hospitality. Soon, these visits became weekly affairs. Paro did not live alone; there was a middle-aged man who lived in the house. He was twice her size and looked more of a minder than a husband, though he probably was the latter. Pai used to boast about his visits to Paro's; and Vacha and I used to laugh at his foolishness, but it had no effect on him whatsoever. A number of times, I joked about his crush on Paro in her presence, but she was not offended and kept smiling. It was the same smile that had made half the men in Meerut lose their heads over her.

Paro was not like other women of the bazaar. She had none of the brashness or vulgarity one normally associated with her professional sisters. Paro was now perfectly at home in the studio and had the confidence to hold her own in sophisticated company and make cultured conversation. One reason for her impeccable manners was the high-grade clientele she entertained in Meerut. It often happens in the film world that newcomers, if they are women, are immediately taken under the wing of one or the other of the old hands, but it did not happen to Paro because Filmistan had a more 'moral' atmosphere than most other studios. Paro, on her part, was in no hurry to get involved with anyone. Among the people there, Mohsin Abdullah, tired of his monotonous, dry bachelor life, was trying to start something with the Parsi girl Veera, who was also a new arrival. Mohsin no longer travelled with us by second class but invariably bought a first-class ticket to share the ride with Veera. She had a dog and Mohsin would often find himself walking her dog in and out of the train. Vacha was not interested in women. He had just got rid of his ill-reputed French wife with some difficulty. S. Mukherjee was trying to interest Naseem Bano, the star who was said to have the face of a fairy, so he did not have eyes for anyone, including Paro. Gyan Mukherjee was not into this sort of thing at all. As for me, what I liked about Paro was her lovely skin. When I mentioned this to my fellow-writer and friend Shahid Latif, he said, 'You like her skin, but do you know what lies under it?' Only Pai was completely out of control. One day, Paro invited him over and poured two large pegs of Johnny Walker for him with her own dainty hands. The whisky travelled to his head right away and Paro gently made him lie on the sofa and doze off, which convinced him that Paro was in love with him, and that we who had failed were jealous. What Paro thought of this fantasy, we did not know.

The shooting of *Shikari* was proceeding well. Veera was the heroine, while Paro had the side role, playing a Burmese tribal girl from the heart of the jungle who is feline and coquettish. I was a bit apprehensive about her acting abilities and began to get nervous as the time to shoot her scenes came closer. I was not sure she could do it. I recall clearly the day her first scene was to be shot. She was all made-up and costumed in a tight bra with a part of her midriff showing and her skirt hanging several inches above her ankles. She did not look in the least scared by the bright lights and the camera. She knew her lines and we were all hoping she would not fumble with them. However, when the time came for the 'take' she suddenly froze, becoming wooden. When she delivered her lines, she did so flatly. We put her through several rehearsals but she remained wooden and lifeless. She would raise her eyebrows like professional dancing girls as if she were quoting a price for her services, but she just could not manage the scene. After four retakes, I began to lose hope. Vacha was the kind to get worried rather quickly and said to me that there was nothing right about her and that S. Mukherjee would have to find some way to deal with the situation.

Mukherjee also tried, but what could he do? That was the way she was. Finally, one take, which was somewhat better, was approved so that we could go on to the next scene. Meanwhile, we were all trying to make her less wooden but we were getting nowhere. It was not that she had any fear of the camera or the microphone; it was only that when the time came, she froze. We had not written her off and were still hopeful that she would get over this problem. Since I was the one who had the least hope in her, I began to rewrite her role so that she would be called upon to do very little by way of acting. She found this out through Pai and after a couple of days I noticed that she was spending much of her spare time chatting me up. She talked well, in a very cultured way. She made no attempt to flatter me but, once or twice, she invited me to her place; I would have gone but I was too busy and obsessed with the revised screenplay of the movie. I had help in the form of Raja Mehdi Ali Khan, Mohsin Abdullah and Dixit, but while Raja had no time because most of it was spent writing letters to his estranged wife, Mohsin was busy chasing Veera, which left Dixit who, poor fellow, would make honest efforts to make Paro speak her lines properly, but without success.

In the meantime, I had begun to notice that when Ashok and Paro did a scene, she gave him looks which clearly implied that if he wanted to do in real life what was being shot for the screen she was willing. Ashok was always a shy person and could never bring himself to declare love to a woman, though I knew that he found Paro attractive. He simply did not have the courage to grab her and take her to bed. So many women had come into his life and he could have become another Lord Byron, but because of his basic shyness, he had always ended up running for the door. In those days, Ashok could have tried his luck with any actress and succeeded with most. I was not surprised that Paro had developed an interest in him. She was new and if her name came to be linked with Ashok's she could become well known very quickly. In the movie, she played a wild, headstrong and aggressive tribal girl who was in love with Ashok, who, in turn, was in love with the other woman, Veera. One outdoor shot involved two boats, in one of which we were going to show Ashok and in the other, Paro. What Paro was expected to do was to jump into Ashok's boat when the two boats drew close and touched. The water was deep and during the take, as she jumped, Ashok's boat suddenly swung away and she fell. Vacha screamed and two or three people jumped after her and pulled her out. She was not scared and, as soon as her clothes were dry, she said she was ready for a retake.

When she was squeezing water out of her clothes, Ashok and I caught sight of her leg all the way up to the thigh. When we had packed up and were driving home, Ashok said to me, 'Manto, that was quite a leg. I felt like roasting it and eating it.' Ashok normally kept his feelings hidden but this time he had spoken his mind. We were in Ashok's MG, as we were every day, and we always went past the street where Paro lived. That evening as we drove by that point, Ashok stopped the car. 'What is it?' I asked. He told me that Paro had thrown a party as it was Holi, and he had been invited. 'Should I go or not?' he asked. 'Go,' I answered. 'You come too,' he suggested. 'Why should I? She has not invited me,' I responded. 'So what?' he said as he turned the car around, coming to a stop in front of her flat, and honked. We looked up and saw Vacha and Pai on her balcony. When Pai saw me, he said, 'Oh, you too are here.' 'Come Dadamoni, we were all waiting for you,' Vacha shouted to Ashok.

Paro was wearing much finery, not something she did normally. She rose as we entered and apologized to me for having forgotten to invite me. Drinks were brought out and just one was enough to send Pai reeling. Vacha asked Paro to sing something but she looked suggestively at Ashok and asked, 'Ashok sahib, would you like me to sing?' Ashok became self-conscious and replied with his usual awkwardness, 'If you sing, I will listen.' She began with a thumri, followed it up with a ghazal and then a film song. Her husband, or whoever he was, kept filling our glasses with whisky and soda. Two drinks and Pai was almost asleep. Ashok was never much of a drinking man and did not take more than a peg and a half. Vacha placed his hand over his glass after his third. Paro concluded with a Hindu devotional song, a bhajan. She must have realized that I was a Muslim and began to sing a naat, a composition in praise of the Holy Prophet. I stopped her, 'Paro Devi, this is a party . . . we are all drinking. I think it may be better that we do not refer to the black-cloaked-one.'[1] She realized her faux pas and apologized.

The food was excellent. Ashok ate quickly and wanted to wash his hands. Paro led him to the bathroom. When he returned, he looked jumpy and ill at ease. 'Let's go, Manto,' he said. We did not talk on the way and he dropped me home. The shooting meanwhile was proceeding according to schedule. One evening when Ashok and I were in his car driving past Shivaji Park where Paro lived, he slowed down and said, 'Manto, let me tell you an interesting story.' His voice trembled a little. 'Do you remember when we went to Paro's and she said she would show me to the bathroom when I wanted to wash my hands?' 'I do,' I replied. 'When she was handing me a towel, she said in a quiet voice, "Tomorrow come all by yourself at six thirty in the evening." It made me so nervous that I dropped the towel and rushed back to the living room.' At this point, he stopped the car.

'Did you go?' I asked. 'Yes . . .' He lifted his hands from the steering wheel, 'but I ran away again.' 'I want the entire story,' I said. 'You know I am a coward,' Ashok continued. 'God knows what comes over me on such occasions. She made me sit on a sofa and sat herself on the floor and snuggled up to me. She poured me two drinks and took a small one herself. Then she began to express her love for me. As I listened to her, I got more and more nervous by the minute. When she grabbed my hand and pressed it, I shook it free. I could see tears in her eyes, but they disappeared almost immediately and she began to smile. "Ashok bhaiyya, I was only testing you," she simpered. I almost

---

[1]Black-cloaked-one is an affectionate reference to the Holy Prophet, who often threw a black cloak over his shoulders.

fell back. "Ashok sahib, I take you as my brother," she said as I got up to leave. I did not say anything and left. When I got home, I took a small drink and felt sorry for myself. I mean where was the harm in it?' 'Yes, there was no harm in it,' I said. His tone became even more wistful. 'And . . . I even liked her.'

My mind went back to the scene we had shot the very day this incident had taken place. It was cold and we were filming outdoors. Everyone was dancing, including Ashok who had his arms around his beloved, Veera. Away from the merrymakers stood Paro, all by herself, looking very sad.

NUR JEHAN: ONE IN A MILLION

I think I first saw Nur Jehan in *Khandan*. She was certainly no 'baby' then, no sir, by no stretch of imagination. She was as well stacked as a young woman would wish to be with the assets women bring into play when required by the situation. To the moviegoers of those days, Nur Jehan was provocative, a ticking bombshell for whom they pined. Speaking for myself, I never found any such appeal in her. To me, there was just one thing about her that was phenomenal—her voice. After Saigal, she was the only singer who impressed me. Her voice was as pure as crystal. Even the suggestion of a note was discernible when she sang, perfectly in command whether the notes she employed were in the lowest range, the middle ones or the highest. I was sure, if she so wished, she could stay on the same note for hours, like those street performers who can walk the entire length of a tightly stretched rope with perfect poise and the greatest ease.

In later years, her voice lost the resonance, richness and innocence that were once its hallmark, but Nur Jehan remained Nur Jehan. Lata Mangeshkar may have captivated the world but Nur Jehan only had to strike a note to make you sit up. Not many people know that she was as conversant with the intricacies of classical music as any acknowledged maestro, being equally adept at singing thumri, khayal and even dhrupad—the last form with an authority that was astonishing. Music was bound to be in her bones because of the family and the surroundings in which she was born, but she spent years learning it. Her talent, there can be no question, was God-given. Technically, a singer may be the most adept but if the voice lacks 'juice', technical knowledge alone cannot move the listener. Nur Jehan had both knowledge and a God-given voice. When these two things come together, the total effect is dazzling.

While one would think that a natural gift is always well looked after, often it is the other way round. Most gifted people are indifferent to their gift and, in fact, try consciously or otherwise to destroy it. Liquor is bad for the throat but the late K.L. Saigal drank heavily all his life. Sour and oily things are bad for the voice but who does not know that Nur Jehan ate large quantities of pickles in oil and, interestingly enough, when she had to record a song, she practically feasted on pickles, followed by iced water. Then and only then did she go and stand in front of the microphone. She had a theory about it. She believed that such things sharpened and enlivened the voice. How that is possible, only she could explain. I may add though that I have seen Ashok Kumar munching ice, especially when he had to record a song. Whatever the secret, as long as there is recorded music, the voice of K.L. Saigal will live, and so will that of Nur Jehan, delighting generation after generation of listeners.

I had seen Nur Jehan only on the screen, never in person. I was a fan, not of her looks, but of her talent as a singer. She was young and it always astonished me how she could sing in such a masterly way. In those days, there were two big names in Indian film music: Saigal and Nur Jehan. There was also Khurshid who had her own following, and much praise was heaped on Shamshad. But the fact is that once Nur Jehan came on the scene, all voices except hers were, so to speak, lowered. Suraiya arrived later. It will always be my great regret that while Saigal and Suraiya were brought together in one movie (*Parwana* with music by Khwaja Khurshid Anwar), it never occurred to any producer to team up Saigal and Nur Jehan. For some reason, the two never worked in a film together. Had they sung together, it would have wrought a delightful revolution in the world of music.

How, when and where I met Nur Jehan for the first time is a long story. After spending many years in Bombay, for certain personal reasons, I had moved to Delhi in a none-too-happy mental state and found a job with All India Radio, but before long I got bored. Meanwhile, Nazir Ludhianwi, editor of the weekly *Mussawar*, had been pestering me in letter after letter to return to Bombay because the man who had directed the recent hit movie *Khandan*, Syed Shaukat Hussain Rizvi, was now in Bombay and staying with him, and was keen that I should write a story for him. So I left Delhi. The political situation in India was turbulent. The Cripps Cabinet Mission had failed and gone back. I think I arrived in Bombay on 7 August 1940 and my first meeting with Shaukat took place at 17 Adelphi Chambers, Clare Road, which served as both his office and his residence.

He was a tall and dashing young man, fair with pink cheeks, a fine John-Gilbert-style moustache and curly hair, extremely well dressed in his spotless, well ironed trousers and a jacket set off with a jauntily knotted tie. He even walked stylishly. We became friends from the word go.

I found him to be a sincere person. I had brought a good stock of my favourite Craven A cigarettes from Delhi because, on account of the war, they were hard to find, especially in Bombay. When Shaukat saw my hoard of over twenty tins and nearly fifty packs, he was delighted. I moved into 17 Adelphi Chambers. We had two huge rooms, one serving as the office, the other as our living quarters, though we always ended up sleeping in the office. Mirza Musharraf, the comedian, and some others would drop in during the evening and before leaving they would make our beds. We were having a great time. There were the Craven A cigarettes and the Deer brand Nasik whisky which was quite atrocious, but which was all we could obtain. Although Shaukat had become a big director after the success of *Khandan*, his long stay in Lahore after the success of the movie had accounted for all the money he had made. Life in Lahore was full of action and, consequently, expensive. All I had was a few hundred rupees, which I had already sunk in Nasik whisky.

However, we managed somehow through those unsettled times. I remember that two days after my arrival in Bombay, on 9 August, the year being 1940, when I tried to make a phone call, the line was dead. We learnt later that, since the leaders of the Indian National Congress were being arrested, city phone lines had been made non-operational as a precautionary measure. Gandhiji, Jawaharlal Nehru, Abul Kalam Azad and other leaders had all been arrested and taken to some unknown place. The city felt like a cocked gun that could go off any moment, so there was no question of going out. For several days, we were cooped up inside, trying to kill time by drinking that dreadful Deer brand whisky. Because of political uncertainty, the film industry had suffered badly, with no one willing to invest money in a new production. The people Shaukat had been negotiating with had let things drift, waiting for more settled times. Meanwhile, we were eating the bad food sent to us by Nazir Ludhianwi and sleeping until late in the morning. Off and on, we would get excited and start talking about new film scripts.

It was during those days that someone told me about Nur Jehan's presence in Bombay. Now, who told me that? My memory appears to be failing me, but I think I knew on 8 August, which was before I met Shaukat, that she was in the city. I wanted to go to Mahim to meet some relatives and also to find out what had become of Samina, who later had an affair with Krishan Chander. She was a radio artist I had met in Delhi at All India Radio. She wanted to get into the movies and I had given her letters for Prithviraj and Brij Mohan. She was bright, good-looking and could speak her lines fluently. I was keen to know if she had been given a break or not. I was fairly confident though that she would make it.

Someone told me that she lived at Shivaji Park but it was such a sprawling neighbourhood that with just her name, Samina Khatoon, to guide me, I could never have hoped to find her. I remembered that Nizami, whose wife Geeta Nizami became a famous movie actress and who married a string of men after she left him, lived at Shivaji Park. It was the same Nizami who had trained Mumtaz Shanti, overseen her career and taught her the ways of the world. Geeta Nizami, I should add, was later involved in many court cases. In the early years of Pakistan, she organized a dance troupe, with a young and lovely woman as her lead dancer, which had performed from city to city. So far Nizami and I had only exchanged letters, and formal ones at that. Were I to really describe our first meeting, it would run into ten to fifteen pages, so I will be brief. When I appeared at his place at

Shivaji Park that morning, he let me in with great warmth. He was wearing just a vest and a dhoti. He asked what had brought me to him and when I told him, he replied, 'Samina Khatoon, I will have her here in no time.' He had an emaciated Hindu manager whom he summoned. 'Get hold of Samina Khatoon and bring her to Manto sahib right away.' After he had issued this order, he assured me that there was nothing he would not do for me. Then he offered to me—in words only, of course—not only a fine, expensively furnished flat but also a car to go with it.

I thanked him for his kind thoughts in appropriate words, which he did not seem to need as he was a fan of my short stories. Nizami, who was as generous as a king when it came to empty promises, has been called all kinds of names, from procurer to pimp, but that was not my problem. I know that he was a man in search of new challenges and in that art he had no equal. I observed that day how total his hold on Mumtaz Shanti was. She was utterly under his influence, as if he were her father. Wali sahib, the director, practically danced around him, like a groom around his mounted master. In that house, Nizami was king and everybody paid him homage. His only duty was to invite producers to parties where good food was served and liquor flowed freely. He was without an equal when it came to buying petrol in the black market. He would spend time teaching Mumtaz Shanti how to become a successful actress. 'Look, if you smile in a certain way, I promise to get you a contract out of that producer,' or, 'If you shake that fat financier's hand the way I teach you, I assure you that we shall have ten thousand rupees in our pocket the same evening.'

I just sat there and wondered at the world into which I had accidentally found my way. Everything about it was artificial. At one point, Nizami asked Wali sahib to bring him his bedroom slippers, which he did and placed the pair at his feet with the utmost reverence. This, I can swear, was an unnatural gesture, something totally insincere. Mumtaz Shanti, wearing the most humdrum clothes, was in the next room hammering nails into a window with Nizami carrying on a running commentary, 'Manto sahib, this child is so simple that although she is in the world of movies, she is unaware of the ways of the world in which we all live. She does not even look at men. And it is all because of the training I have given her.' While I knew that this was all untrue, I could not help admiring Nizami. But let me get back to Nur Jehan.

After Nizami told me how he had put Mumtaz Shanti on the road to success and how exquisitely he had trained her, Nur Jehan's name came up. He said she, too, was under his tutelage and was learning the ropes like Mumtaz Shanti. I recall his words: 'Manto sahib, had this girl stayed on in Lahore, it would have been her end. I have had her come out here and I have impressed upon her that it is not enough to become a film star. There should be other means of support and security for a girl. There is no need to get into any kind of love affair in the beginning. What she should do is earn as much as she can from all possible sources and when she has enough money in the bank she can pick up a nice man and marry him so that he remains a slave to her all his life. What do you think, Manto sahib? You are a very wise man.'

What wisdom I might have had had abandoned me the moment I stepped into Nizami's flat. I had no answer to his question, so I told him that whatever he was doing appeared to be right and how could it be otherwise, since it was he who was doing it. That pleased him greatly, so he sent for Nur Jehan. We heard the phone ring in the next room, followed by Nur Jehan's voice. 'It is Kamal sahib on the line. I will be with you shortly,' Nizami smiled mysteriously. The Kamal on the line was Syed Kamal Amrohi, famous since the film *Pukar*,[1] which he had directed. Nizami spoke, 'I was telling you about my advice to her. I have drilled it into her that this marriage business is neither here nor there; she should do the best by herself first. Now Kamal can earn. If half of what he earns comes to Nur Jehan, wouldn't that be the best for her? The fact, Manto sahib, the fact is that

---

[1]Kamal Amrohi did not direct the film *Pukar*. He wrote it. Sohrab Modi is credited with its direction.

these actresses should become adept in the art of earning money.'

'With teachers like you, they can't miss,' I said with a smile. This made him happy and he ordered one first-rate lemonade for me. So this was where Nur Jehan was being trained and educated in a scientific manner. She was being taught all the tricks of the trade under Nizami's personal supervision. Nur Jehan, having finished her call, came into the room and we met, but casually. It was my impression that this girl was growing into womanhood rapidly and the smile on her lips and her laughter were already quite commercial. She also seemed to have a tendency to become plump. But there was no doubt that she was going to prove the most talented student Nizami had ever had.

However, fate had other things in mind. It was Nizami's desire that, like Mumtaz Shanti, Nur Jehan too should remain under his thumb and accept his authority. He was like a retired madam who wanted this young woman to be a part of his establishment. Everything that Mumtaz Shanti earned, for example, remained in Nizami's custody. It was obvious that compared to Mumtaz Shanti's market value, Nur Jehan's was far greater. Nizami was too wily a man not to know that a great future lay in wait for this girl. It was only natural that he should be keen to keep this butterfly in his net.

Shaukat had had an affair with Nur Jehan in Lahore's Pancholi Studio (where *Khandan* was filmed). There was even a court case in the course of which Nur Jehan had testified that she had had no intimate relations with Shaukat who was like a brother to her. This court brother of hers was now in this vast city of Bombay, the Hollywood of India. When I told Shaukat later that I had met Nur Jehan, I did not know about their affair, nor did I know that their present relations were bad. I just told him that I had met her at Nizami's house. It was nothing more than a minor piece of interesting gossip. No sooner had the words left my lips that he banged the glass containing that dreadful Deer brand whisky on the table and exclaimed, 'Let her go to hell!' Lightly, I replied, 'I am quite happy with that but remember she played the heroine in your *Khandan*.' Shaukat understood my pun—'khandan' being family in Urdu—and said, 'Manto, you are a mischievous man, but it is like this. I just do not want to know anything about her. Of course, she is in Bombay, the sali has chased me all the way here, but I wish to have nothing to do with her.'

When I told him that she was on the phone to Kamal Amrohi and that Nizami was trying to get the two together, he pretended not to care but I knew that it had hit him hard. He at once commissioned Mirza Musharraf to go out and get another pint of Deer brand whisky and we kept drinking till late into the night. In between, after long gaps, the name of Nur Jehan would come up and it was clear to me that Shaukat was still smitten by her. The brother bit was no more than legal hair-splitting. He was still thinking of those nights when this little princess of song used to be in his arms with both of them promising each other eternal love. One day, rather abruptly, I asked Shaukat, 'Confess . . . aren't you in love with Nur Jehan?' Shaukat flicked the ash off his cigarette and replied self-consciously, 'I am . . . but the hell with her. I will get over her in time.' That, however, was not what fate intended.

Shaukat was offered a contract by Seth V.M. Vyas, owner of Sunrise Pictures, which he accepted. Vyas had earlier signed Nur Jehan for one of his movies. A word about Vyas. He started out as a tabla player, graduated to a camera coolie and became a cameraman. The next anybody knew, he was a director and with another leap, a producer in the big league. He was so thin that he would always wear a thick vest under his shirt so that no one could see his ribcage. There was no question that he was a smart fellow who worked hard at his job. He could go on from morning until night without showing the least sign of fatigue. One thing more about Vyas. He never used his own money to make a movie. After completing one film, he would announce another and sign up a star-studded cast. At that stage, there would be nothing to the movie at all, not even a story or a financier. However, sure enough, someone would swallow the dangling bait of the star cast and Vyas would ask him to put his money up front so that work could begin. Seth Vyas would then start production after having thanked the goddess Kali whose devotee he was.

As soon as Nur Jehan landed in Bombay, he signed her up because he knew that after the success of *Khandan* her name would attract many financiers. And when he realized that the movie director was also in town, he sent his men after him, held many meetings with him and, finally, signed him up to direct his forthcoming film.

No one knew what sort of movie was in the offing or what its story would be. However, when Vyas waved around the contracts he had signed with Shaukat and Nur Jehan, he was able to raise the money without the least difficulty. Destiny sometimes plays strange games. Shaukat did not know that Nur Jehan had come to Sunrise Pictures, nor was she aware that the man she had described as 'my brother' in a Lahore court was also in the same company now.

Their coming together could not have remained a secret for very long, and when it got out, it had Nizami worried because it threatened to jeopardize his plans for Nur Jehan and Kamal Amrohi. Invoking his rights as Nur Jehan's 'guardian', he informed Seth Vyas that the teaming up of the two was unacceptable to him. However, Vyas being a Gujarati—a far smarter breed than Punjabis can ever be—talked him into giving his blessing to the arrangement. In fact, then Nizami became so enthusiastic about Nur Jehan's working in Shaukat's film that he declared Vyas to be his brother and shook hands with him on the deal with great feeling, at the latter's office.

Both of them were now happy for their own reasons: Vyas because he had got what he wanted and Nizami because he had won the goodwill of a rich and resourceful man. Seth Vyas was a strict Vaishnavite, or else the same evening Nizami would have invited him over and made him feast on chicken curry and pulao prepared by Mumtaz Shanti with her own dainty hands. Had the Seth been a drinking man, Nizami would have sent out his emaciated manager and asked him to procure two bottles of Scotch from the black market. Any way, the deal was done and

Nizami had placed his hand on his heart and declared to Vyas, 'Seth, now that you have called me your brother, you have my word that come hell or high water, Baby Nur Jehan will be on your set when required.'

Meanwhile, I had also signed a contract with Seth Vyas to write a story, and Shaukat and I were trying to decide what it should be. We had received our advances and if there was one thing which was not in short supply it was Nasik's Deer brand whisky. Mirza Musharraf, the comedian, Chawla and Saigal (both were to become well known film directors) would often be in attendance. Chawla would go running to Nagpada if we ran out of whisky; and if there were other errands, there was always Mirza Musharraf. After three drinks, he would invariably start crying, kiss Shaukat's hands and beg him for forgiveness for whatever he thought he had done against Shaukat in the past. 'All false, all false,' he would say. Then he would cry for his newly acquired wife and follow it with singing. It was all a masquerade but then that's what the world of films is.

Seth Vyas, meanwhile, had begun shooting his film, but none of the scenes so far had involved Nur Jehan, which meant that Shaukat and she were yet to get together. One day there was a notice on the studio bulletin board that Nur Jehan would be shooting that night. It just happened that I was at Shivaji Park where my good friend and the famous music director Rafiq Ghaznavi lived. Ghaznavi had a romance knotted into every necktie he possessed—and his collection was large. He was a friend of mine and there was no formality between us. When I arrived at his flat, I found a full house. On a sofa sat his latest wife, Khurshid alias Anuradha, and next to her was Nur Jehan. Nizami was in a chair, and Rafiq Ghaznavi was on the floor appearing to get ready to attack a latter-day Somnath in the tradition of his ancestor Mahmud of Ghazni who had invaded and ransacked the famous Hindu temple at Somnath.

I was not sure whether Rafiq was planning an 'invasion' on Nur Jehan or if Nizami or Nur Jehan suspected anything. God alone knows. Nizami told me that Mumtaz Shanti was also expected any minute. I was a bit mystified. How could this great drinking party be in full swing when there was to be a shoot at the studio? Nizami held a glass in his hand and Nur Jehan had a glass of some colourful liquid in hers, which she was sipping daintily. Khurshid alias Anuradha was taking long swigs like a seasoned drinker and as for Rafiq from Ghazni— the land which had given birth to Mahmud who had fallen in love with a boy called Ayaz—he was telling dirty stories. He had sworn at me in his fulsome way, which was his usual manner of greeting, but had changed tack immediately and said politely, 'Please, my dear, come and sit here.' He looked at Nur Jehan and asked me, 'Do you know her?' 'I know her,' I replied. Rafiq was never able to take more than four drinks. He obviously had already done that because he said to me in a slurred voice, 'No, you know nothing, Manto. This is Nur . . . Nur Jehan . . . Nur means light and she is not only the light of the world but also the spirit's elixir. By God, she has a voice sweeter than that of any houri in paradise. Were a houri to hear her sing, she would be so jealous that she would rush to earth and give her something to drink to destroy her vocal chords.'

I knew why he was building these bridges of praise. He wanted to employ them later to walk across to her bed. I noticed that Nur Jehan was not much interested in him. She was listening to him though, and off and on, she would flash an insincere smile at him. Rafiq was a great miser but that day he was overly generous. He poured a large drink from the bottle for me and insisted that I gulp it down in one go, so that he could give me another. Everyone was drinking, but Nur Jehan's drink was the lightest and she was sucking at it as honey bees suck honey from flowers. Rafiq had not stopped building his bridges of praise although his earlier structures had all collapsed. Suddenly, the phone rang.

Khurshid picked up the receiver with her delicate hand and looked upset. Then she placed her hand on the mouthpiece and whispered that it was Seth Vyas on the line wondering where Nur Jehan was. 'Dear daughter, tell him that Nur Jehan is not here,' Nizami said, which was what Khurshid told Vyas in more or less appropriate words. 'Sheedan,' Rafiq said to Khurshid as soon as she was off the phone, 'go get the harmonium . . . Seth Vyas can go to hell.' She went into another room and was soon back with a harmonium. Rafiq pushed back the top, pumped the bellows and struck a note. It was his style that, with his eyes half-shut, he would begin to swoon over the note he had just emitted from his throat. 'Hai . . . God be praised . . . Oh,' he kept saying. Every note seemed to send him into ecstasy. That was his technique. He would have his listeners applauding long before the performance had begun. But he did not sing that day because all his concentration was on Nur Jehan. At one point, he struck a note and with his half-dilated eyes said to her, 'Nur . . . sing something . . . Oh! What a divine note!'

You may have seen actors and actresses playing roles on the screen but let me take you to this live show. Nur Jehan lifted the harmonium and placed it next to her on the sofa. Khurshid came and sat beside her, holding a half-empty glass of whisky. Rafiq Ghaznavi was squatting on the floor, looking at Nur Jehan with his love-sick eyes, swaying his body and shaking his head even before she had opened her mouth. On a chair sat Nizami and next to him, this old sinner, nursing his second drink.

Nur Jehan began to sing. It was a thumri in the raag Piloo, *Toray nainaan kalar bin karey*—no antimony do your black eyes need. Then we all heard a car drive into the porch. The man who got down and walked straight in was none other than Seth Vyas. For a moment everybody was taken aback but Nizami quickly got the situation under control. He pretended that he had not seen Vyas come in and shouted at Khurshid, 'What do you think you are doing? Don't you see in what great pain she is and here you are trying to force her to sing . . . Look, she has hardly sung one line and it looks as if she is going to faint.' Then he looked at Nur Jehan and said in a worried voice, 'Lie down, Nur Jehan, lie down.' He did not wait for her to do so, but stepped forward to help her recline on the sofa. Nur Jehan began to moan loudly as if she were in great pain. Rafiq also got up, trying to look concerned. Nizami spoke to Khurshid next, 'What are you waiting for, Sheedan? Go and get her a hot-water bottle. That is a bad fit she is having.'

Sheedan went into the next room, taking quick steps. Nizami tried to calm Nur Jehan, who had now begun to wail softly, then he sat next to Seth Vyas and said, 'She has been in terrible pain since yesterday. She said to me, "Uncle, I don't think I can make it to the shooting." But I told her, "No, little one, this would be a bad omen. This is your first picture in Bombay and the first day of shooting . . . but forget that . . . What matters is that I have called Seth Vyas my brother . . . and you have to go even if you die." So we came here to get some brandy from Rafiq which might help her, and also to ask him to have his car drop us at the studio . . . you are my brother, Seth.'

Seth Vyas kept quiet, as did everyone else. Rafiq was chewing his nails and I, glass in hand, was wondering what it was all about. The story of the movie was mine, the music that of Rafiq Ghaznavi, and Seth Vyas, our boss, had caught us in the act, as it were, what with the drinks and the music. Nizami kept talking to Seth Vyas, assuring him that since they were now brothers there should be no misgivings between them. Khurshid appeared with a hot-water bottle, which she placed on Nur Jehan's stomach, and she pretended that it somewhat soothed her pain. Nizami now said to Vyas, who had begun to look more and more like the sphinx, 'You don't have to stay for this. Rafiq and I will bring Nur Jehan over to the studio.' Then he said in a loud aside. 'I think Khurshid should come along too. Women know what these women's things are.' Seth Vyas rose, put his cap on and walked out. Everyone heaved a sigh of relief. Nur Jehan put aside the hot-water bottle, which actually contained cold water, and said to Nizami, 'But uncle Nizami, hadn't you told me not to go today?' Nizami became serious. 'Little one, look, I said that for your own good. If you go on the first day without the producer coming in person to fetch you, he will start taking you for granted. Ask Mumtaz. She never goes unless the studio sends her a car, and when it comes I let the driver wait for at least an hour, although Rai Bahadur Chunilal is such a good friend of mine. I don't really care. Many times, he has had to come personally to fetch Mumtaz. Don't worry, everything is in order now. Vyas came himself to fetch you. You are very sick but you are going despite being sick. Seth Vyas will remember that.'

Nizami spent some more time explaining the delicate relationship between producer and artist. The conversation began to slowly veer towards Shaukat Hussain Rizvi. Nizami seemed keen to impress on Nur Jehan that she should have nothing more to do with Shaukat and there should be no place in her heart for him. She should follow the same path as Mumtaz Shanti had done all along under his guidance, with such successful results. I butted in at this point because Shaukat was a friend and he had told me that he was in love with Nur Jehan. It was also clear to me that the various women who were brought to him by Mirza Musharraf were needed because Shaukat was trying to bury Nur Jehan's memory in their warm embrace. He was also drinking that third-class Deer brand whisky to forget the woman with whom he was really in love.

Shaukat was like a watchmaker, a man perfect at his craft. He was always putting things right. Even if they were right, he had to put them just right. By temperament, he had no patience with anything that did not work, such as a nail which had not been pushed into a wall straight, a watch that did not keep correct time, or a pair of trousers that needed the touch of a hot iron. He was instinctively organized and disciplined, the same factors that make a watch keep good time. However, when it came to Nur Jehan, he felt helpless. How could he set right the watch that they call the heart? Had it been something he could have examined under a magnifying glass, he would have taken it to pieces and then put it back together so that it worked to perfection. This was an entirely different matter.

And there was Nur Jehan who could produce the most perfect note from her throat but who found herself unable to make Shaukat depart from her heart. She could sing the khayal with the ease of a maestro but the only thing on her mind these days was the young and willowy Shaukat, who had given her the most joyful moments of her life, who had sent a tingle through her body that the finest music had been unable to transmit. How could she forget the man who had given her such perfect physical fulfilment?

When I mentioned Shaukat to her, Nur Jehan pretended that she did not care for him. 'Look here, Nur Jehan, that's nonsense. That's not how you feel, and what that ass Shaukat tells me, I don't believe a word of it either. You are head over heels in love with each other, but you are bent upon pretending otherwise. Only yesterday we sat talking about you in the office of the magazine *Mussawar* and the day before, and the day before. Whenever Shaukat and I drink in the evening, on one excuse or another, he drags your name into the conversation. You are no different. I think I saw your eyes go wet once or twice when you mentioned his name. He is in the same state, I can tell you. I think this is no good and I am convinced that Shaukat cannot do without you. What kind of a spell have you cast on him?'

Nur Jehan listened to me as if she were in a trance. 'Look, Nur Jehan,' I added, 'don't deceive yourself. I know that Nizami sahib is a man of much worldly wisdom and the methods that he advocates may work in other departments of life; but when it comes to love, they will prove to be fake coins.' I turned towards Nizami and asked, 'Is it untrue?' He was so absorbed in what I was saying that he shook his head in an emphatic 'no'. When he realized that he had erred by agreeing with me, it was too late. I could see tears in Nur Jehan's eyes. I carried on, 'Both of you are fools. You love each other but try to hide it. From whom, may I ask? This world, Nur Jehan, cannot bear to see two people in love, but does that mean people should stop falling in love? Mumtaz Shanti's life is worth envying, I concede, and I have no doubt that under the benevolent care of her uncle Nizami she will go far.' At this point, I turned towards Nizami again. 'But you must know, Nizami sahib, that you cannot be everyone's uncle. The advice you have been giving Mumtaz may not necessarily be good for Nur Jehan. They are two different people. Am I wrong?'

I had brought Nizami to a point where he could not say no to anything I was saying. I kept talking and by the time I was done I had convinced Nur Jehan that Shaukat and she were made for each other and it was silly of them to pretend otherwise. When Nizami rose to leave, he was not a happy man. He must have been angry with me but it was not in his nature to show that. All he could do was instruct Nur Jehan that she should go to the studio with Khurshid with a hot- rather than a cold-water bottle. She was also told to complain about her 'pain' at regular intervals. He asked me about my living arrangements and assured me that he would soon have me move into a properly furnished flat, which he had already found. In fact, the key was with his manager and all I had to do was call him. If I needed petrol from the black market, it would be available too. He assured me that he sincerely wished me to accept his offer and promised to entertain me soon with roast chicken and Johnny Walker Black Label. I thanked him and declined but he was insistent that I should accept his offers. So I said yes, but I knew that the next time I went to visit him, there would be no roast chicken or Black Label whisky waiting for me. One thing was clear: I had upset Nizami's apple cart that evening.

I also learnt in the next few days that Nur Jehan had no interest in the film director Kamal Amrohi. She had been refusing to take his phone calls. When he drove up to Nizami's place in his second-hand car, she would hide in another room to avoid him. Whatever I learnt about her, I dutifully conveyed to Shaukat, though we both knew that it would not be easy to cut her loose from the old sorcerer Nizami. Finally, we held a conference, which included Nazir Ludhianwi, editor of *Mussawar*, at which it was decided to rent a flat on Cadell Road close to the beach. We were lucky to find one on the ground floor with three bedrooms, a large living area and a few other rooms. Nazir, who was sick and tired of living in his awful flat at Adelphi Chambers, said he would pay half the rent of the new place which, if I remember, was one hundred and seventy-five or two hundred rupees a month. We brought in furniture and other things and set it up nicely. Shaukat's bedroom faced the sea. Nizami's place was barely five hundred yards away. I was carrying out my 'assignment' effectively, which was to pop into Nizami's flat every now and then and give Nur Jehan the latest details of Shaukat's lovelorn days and nights. I would tell her that all she needed to do was take a walk, which would not only be good for her health but would also do wonders for her love life. Sometimes I felt like an old procuress but then what are friends for?

It is ironic to think that in those days I was dead set against marriage and even more opposed to marrying an actress. I believed that two people who liked each other should live together and go their own separate ways once they were tired of the relationship. However, Shaukat believed in putting things down in black and white so that, like inherited land, it would remain his for the rest of his life. I tried to talk him out of it and succeeded in convincing him that if Nur Jehan came to him he should live with her but not marry her. Having done what I could for my friend Shaukat, I got down to writing the screenplay of *Naukar*, a movie I had been assigned. I lived in Byculla, which was some distance from Cadell Road, which meant that our meetings became infrequent.

It was impossible in those days to get good beer. One day I came upon four magnum-size bottles of American beer and thought of sharing them with Shaukat. It was morning but breakfast with beer was not a bad idea. When I walked into his flat, it looked deserted. Nazir had already left for the day it seemed, so I tiptoed towards Shaukat's bedroom and knocked at the door. There was no answer. I knocked again, this time less gently and heard Shaukat's sleepy voice, 'Who's it?' 'Manto,' I answered. 'Wait,' he said. Three minutes later, the door opened and I saw Nur Jehan lying on the only bed in the room. Her eyes looked fresh, almost laundry-washed. Shaukat appeared to be somewhat tired. 'Has the Chittaur fort fallen?'[2] I asked. Shaukat smiled. 'Come, sit down.' I took a stool that lay in front of the dressing table. Shaukat looked triumphantly at Nur Jehan, who was trying to get under the sheets. 'Came to me tied in thin gossamer thread,' he said. Whether she had come tied in thin gossamer or a sturdier variety of thread, I do not know, but it was clear that whatever the thread, it had been knitted out of

---

[2]Chataur is a pun on the Urdu word for buttocks; Chittaur is the name of a famous Indian fort which fell after a long seige.

love because she had finally leapt across the five-hundred-yard gulf that had separated her from Shaukat all this time.

The long and short of it was that the one item of furniture that Shaukat's flat had lacked was now in place. As for Nizami's flat, a light had gone out of it, a light that could have lit up his entire establishment. Nizami had not given up easily. After doing his best to talk her out of her resolve to go and live with Shaukat, he had called in her brothers, who threatened her with violence if she refused to change her mind. However, nothing had worked, neither counsel nor threats. 'I think I should marry the sali,' Shaukat said to me. 'You decide. She is yours, but in my view that won't be the thing to do. Have you spoken to your family about her?' was my reaction. He did not answer and I left, hoping that he would not act in a hurry.

In those days, there was a character in Bombay by the name of Hakim Abu Mohammad Tahir Ashk Azimabadi. About seventy-five years old, he had the heart of a young man. His eyesight was perfect, his teeth were intact and he had never missed a movie opening night. He spoke five languages—Urdu, Persian, Arabic, English and Punjabi—and was one of a kind. He also dabbled in herbal medicine, wrote poetry and liked the company of friends. I had introduced him to Shaukat, who had taken to him immediately and begun calling him 'uncle'. In fact, he had found some distant family link with the old man. As I said earlier, my visits to Shaukat had become infrequent because of the distance and my work at the studio, but I liked Hakim Tahir and often sought his advice about my prose which he would happily give as he liked me, too. One day I ran into him and was told that Shaukat had married Nur Jehan. I was surprised and showed it. After some hesitation, Hakim Tahir said to me, 'Look Saadat, it was all done very quietly because it is best that people do not know. I have told you because you are like a son to me, just like Shaukat. But keep it to yourself.'

How could I argue with a seventy-five-year-old man that this secret would not remain a secret for very long? I felt a little hurt though that Shaukat had not taken me into confidence. If he wanted to marry her, why was I kept out? Why was I thrown out of the pack like the joker? I was hurt but I never mentioned it to Shaukat because it would have affected our relationship. Time passed. Nizami had given up on Nur Jehan as had Kamal Amrohi after countless unanswered calls and scores of trips to Nizami's flat in his second-hand car. Shaukat's bedroom was alive with life and laughter and the molten music of Nur Jehan's voice. Rafiq Ghaznavi was the film's music director and Nur Jehan would rehearse her songs in Shaukat's seafront love nest.

And now a story. My brother Saeed Hasan, who was a barrister in Fiji, came to Bombay after many years. He was on his way to Amritsar. I was informed that he would be arriving by air. I lived in a tiny flat so my wife and I decided that he should stay at Shaukat and Nazir's place because it had plenty of room. Nazir was a bachelor and all Shaukat seemed to use was the one bedroom in which he had his Nur Jehan. He had no interest in the other rooms. It would be perfectly convenient for them to put up my brother who would welcome a European-style room with an attached bath. When I brought him over he liked it because it was new. The landlord lived on the upper floor and there was a children's play area with a seesaw and slides just a few steps away, which was pleasant to see. The breeze from the sea blew into the rooms at all hours. Sometimes, it would be so strong that the doors and windows had to be kept tightly shut. A few days passed happily but there was trouble in store.

Shaukat was having the time of his life. He had his Nur Jehan as well as his hangers-on—Mirza Musharraf, Chawla and Saigal who were dying to be part of his team. Those who work in the movie industry are night people. During the day they are busy with their different chores but the evenings are for fun and games. Shaukat's place had a party going every evening, with his friends drinking, telling dirty stories, laughing, singing and sometimes making so much noise that the neighbours would protest. One evening Shaukat had the usual crowd over, including M.A. Mugghani—who was known all over Bombay as movie queen Naseem's drumbeater—my wife and myself. We ate and left as we had to go somewhere else. My brother was dining out so he returned late. As he stepped into the front reception area, the party was in full swing. Everyone was drunk and some people were dancing. In other words, a good time was being had by one and all. However, my brother was a serious-minded barrister who lived abroad and was a complete stranger to such goings-on. Next morning, he packed his things and moved into a place called Khilafat House. He also cursed me and my friends without mincing his words. Even today when I think of what he said I feel as if molten lead were being poured into my ears. He had spent his entire life reading his law books and fighting legal battles in Lahore, Bombay, east Africa and the Fiji Islands. How could he know what movies were all about and what kind of people were associated with them? Interestingly enough, Khilafat House was situated in a street called Love Lane.

But let me get back to Nur Jehan. Her elder sister also lived not far from Cadell Road, and she ran a whorehouse with her brother. I am not sure if the two sisters ever met in those days, but I doubt if Shaukat would ever have permitted Nur Jehan to do so. Her brother was an inveterate gambler who played cards, went to the races and had been dead set against his sister marrying Shaukat. He had tried hard with Nizami's help to talk Nur Jehan out of her obsession with Shaukat because, as far as he was concerned, she was the goose who laid the golden eggs. Shaukat was also threatened several times but it had no effect on him. In the end, everyone came to accept that Nur Jehan and Shaukat were together and intended to remain that way. Work on the movie *Naukar* was proceeding at a good pace, but I often felt that Rafiq Ghaznavi looked distinctly unhappy because Nur Jehan, whom he fancied, had been snatched away from under his very nose.

Shaukat was a hard man to please. He liked things done his way. He was never entirely satisfied with assignments carried out by others. I had given him the script and the screenplay, which he had said he liked, but I found out that he had asked various other people to come up with alternatives, including Hakim Tahir. I did not mind him because he was someone I respected as an elder, but I could not tolerate the others. One day I told Shaukat in no uncertain words what I thought of it all. He tried to calm me because he was always a very diplomatic and cool-headed person, but I am by nature obstinate and once my mind is made up nothing can make me change it. In any case, I did not like the story I had written because Shaukat had made me put in several changes of which I did not approve. Although Shaukat was a close friend and we had been drinking that awful Deer brand whisky day after day and smoking Craven A cigarettes, I knew that, though he would do whatever else I asked him to do, insofar as the movie was concerned, he would do exactly what his watchmaker's brain told him to do. I, therefore, walked out of *Naukar* quietly, normally. Shaukat knew me well and may even have welcomed my departure. Had I stayed, I could have delayed the production for several months because we would have argued endlessly.

I was cut up with Shaukat, and he may have felt the same way towards me, but our friendship remained unaffected. The movie industry was by then in trouble because of political uncertainty in the country. All you had to do to kill a handful of films under production was climb on a table and shout 'Long live the revolution'. And because of the Second World War, raw film was hard to come by. It was a very uncertain situation all around. Film directors, in particular, had been hit hard. The producers had a ready excuse to say 'No'. 'Where is the money?' they would ask when approached. There was a war on. It moved from Crete today to Finland tomorrow, and then there was the constant fear of a Japanese invasion of India. However, it was during those uncertain years that capitalists, moneylenders and film producers made their millions.

Shaukat had signed another contract, I think, with Seth Javeri who was a difficult character and, in my view, a third-class person. It was the war that had made him a seth. He had money to burn and he had set up a film company and bought two or three cars. The big actresses were outside his reach, but he had picked up a number of film extras as his women of pleasure. He signed Shaukat up and gave him an advance of Rs 3000. When he cashed the cheque, I was with him. I took him to the post office and made him send all that money to his parents.

Nur Jehan must have hated me for that, but it would not have bothered me. I also persuaded Shaukat to get himself insured. He used to say 'yes' to most things I told him and he agreed to this one as well. I got him a Rs 10,000 policy. Why was I doing all those things? I do not know. I was behaving like an elder of the family, handing out advice to others while taking none myself.

Nur Jehan had blossomed after moving in with Shaukat. It is only physical contact with a man that gives the final touches to a woman's beauty, and by now Nur Jehan was a full-blown woman. The slight, girlish figure she had had in Lahore had been transformed by Bombay. Her body was now privy to all varieties of carnal pleasure and, though some people still called her Baby Nur Jehan, she was no baby, but a woman who had known love and its ecstasy. Shaukat was going to shoot one of the scenes of the movie outdoors in a garden in the suburbs of Bombay. He insisted that I go along. Since it was to appear as a night scene in the film, he was going to shoot it with a red filter on the camera. I got there in Seth Vyas's car. Nur Jehan had already arrived and was wearing a strange outfit, which was a shock to the eyes. Her shalwar was made out of a material called 'net'. Normally, it was used for window sheers but this was what either Shaukat or she had chosen to cover her lower torso. You could say that her shalwar had a thousand tiny windows through which her lower body was streaming. Her shirt was made of the same stuff. Nothing had been left to the imagination. The actress Shobhna Samarth was also present and I walked across to her because, frankly, I found Nur Jehan's dress shocking. Shobhna was an educated woman who knew how to converse. She came from a good Marathi family and there was nothing banal about her. She had superb manners. She was also doing a role in the movie. I sat next to her on the bare grass so that I could regain my composure, which had received a rude shock after one look at Nur Jehan and her vulgar outfit. I had gone there because Shaukat had insisted; otherwise I had no interest in *Naukar*, though I had written it.

I met Nur Jehan several times later at their flat and, when I studied her with more care, I noticed that she had every single characteristic associated with the background from which she came. Everything about her was a put-on. She was flirtatious but not in a cultivated way. I was surprised at how Shaukat, who came from the heart of UP could get along with this diehard peasant Punjabi girl. Shaukat would try to imitate her thick Punjabi-accented Urdu and she would try to imitate his pure UP accent. Shaukat finally completed *Naukar* and we drifted even further apart. Having tasted the joys of love, he was now concentrating on his work, as I was. Off and on, we would run into each other in a film company's office or a studio or on the roadside and exchange greetings, chat for a minute or two and go our separate ways. The movie industry had come out of the doldrums and the war psychosis was gone as far as the producers were concerned. Everyone realized that the industry had entered a boom period.

Shaukat had always had a good head for business. He took advantage of the prevailing state of the market and set up his own production company. He already had an excellent reputation as a director and editor, and his entry into production was bound to put him in the spotlight. Normally, in the film world marriages with actresses are seldom because of love alone. I am not sure if Shaukat felt the same way towards Nur Jehan. What I do know is that even if he had not married her, he would still have done well. He was a man who knew his art and who worked hard. I never understood why he left Bombay to come to Pakistan. Was it because he was always a strict Muslim and could not have countenanced even the least slight to Islam, which he might have had to experience in Bombay after Independence? I am sure if someone had said something against Islam in his presence, he would have unscrewed his skull with one of his implements, taken every piece apart and then put it back after removing the defect that made people say such things. It is also possible that it was Nur Jehan who persuaded him to leave Bombay because she had always loved Lahore: Lahore is Lahore, as all Punjabis say.

In Bombay, Shaukat was highly successful. He had made two runaway hits and he could have stayed there and minted money but he chose Pakistan as his home. Shaukat, a man whose watchmaker's mind could tolerate not the least inefficiency, came to Lahore where the movie industry was on its last legs. He bought the burnt-out Shorey Studios and turned it into a first-class production facility. Few would know that every nail in Shahnoor Studios had been put in there by Shaukat, hammered in securely with his own hands. Every plant in its gardens, and every machine in the laboratory, was put there by Shaukat himself. This is his great quality, though it has not always endeared him to people.

I have a friend in Lahore who often helps me with money. Once I went to see him and found that he had no cufflinks to go with his spotless white shirt. When I expressed surprise, he told me that he had no money to buy them. When I asked him for a cigarette, he replied that for ten days running he had been smoking others' cigarettes. This was the man in whose studio everyone used to be given cool, clean refrigerated water, where flowers bloomed, where scores of gardeners worked, where hundreds of workmen were employed, and where there was a woman called Nur Jehan who wore the most expensive clothes available and who was chauffeured around in limousines. That friend, of course, is Shaukat.

There are many stories about Nur Jehan, some of which may even be true. All I know is that she is the mother of two wonderful boys who are being educated at Chiefs College, Lahore, and whom she loves. Not long ago, there was a variety show at the college where a tableau was presented by the children, with one of Nur Jehan's boys playing the cowherd girl Radha who is in love with Lord Krishna. He had danced beautifully. Nur Jehan knows how to dance. She may even have given a few lessons to the boy Akbar, or maybe it is in his genes. One will have to see what these two boys, Akbar and Asghar, grow up to be. Will this be another family of artists like the Barrymores and the Kapoors? Only time will tell.

Nur Jehan can be arrogant. An arrogance that can't be justified by her looks, as she does not have them in any great measure, but she has a voice, a voice full of light, of which she can be justly proud. I remember once my wife asked me in Bombay if I would ask Nur Jehan to come over as some of her friends wanted to meet her. I told her it should be no problem, and asked Shaukat, who sent Nur Jehan to our place a day later. Of all the actresses I knew—and I knew scores and scores of them—Nur Jehan was the most formal in her manner, always standing on ceremony, always conscious of who she was. Everything about her was affected, her smile, her laughter, the way she greeted people, the way she asked them how they were. Could her married life also be a pretence? I think not. She came and met everyone with her usual affected warmth. I wanted to leave but a friend of my wife's insisted that I stay because she wanted me to request Nur Jehan to sing. 'Let's have a couple of songs,' I said to Nur Jehan with great informality. 'Maybe another time, Manto sahib,' she said in an affected voice. 'My throat is acting up.' I was burnt to a cinder because I know that her throat is fashioned out of steel, which nothing can damage. I knew she was putting on airs. 'This excuse won't work. You will have to sing. I have heard you a thousand times but these people really want to hear you, so whether your throat is acting up or not you should sing something for them,' I said to her.

She said 'No' a few more times, while the women insisted. My wife had had enough. 'Please let's not force her,' she said. But I am not the kind to give up. 'You will have to sing, Nur Jehan,' I said. Finally, she relented and sang Faiz's famous lines, *Aaj ki raat saaz-i-dard na chher*. It was superb. It is years since that happened but I can still feel the golden honey of her voice cascading into my ears.

There are so many men who are in love with Nur Jehan. I know cooks who prepare food for their sahibs and memsahibs while looking longingly at her picture, which they have stuck on the kitchen wall. I also know domestic servants who do not care for Nargis, Nimmi or Kamini Kaushal but who are mad about Nur Jehan. Wherever they see a picture of hers, they clip it and put it in their collection, which they hoard in a broken tin trunk so that they can soothe their eyes by looking at it in their spare hours. Were someone to say something disparaging about Nur Jehan, such men would be prepared to fight. In our own home, we have a lover of Nur Jehan who calls every young girl, every bride and every woman wearing red, 'Nur Jehan'. He knows practically all her songs. He himself is very good-looking so I am at a loss to understand what it is about Nur Jehan that he likes so much that he keeps talking about her from morning to evening.

He is closely related to me, being the son of my nephew Hamid Jalal and my sister-in-law Zakia. His name is Shahid Jalal but we all call him 'Taku'. We have tried to tell him many times that he should seriously think of falling out of love with Nur Jehan whom he cannot marry, as she is already married and has her own children, but it has no effect on him. He loves movies and if these movies do not star Nur Jehan he is very upset. He comes home and begins to sing her songs. He has told his parents that all he wants in the world is Nur Jehan. Some time ago, his grandfather Mian Jalaluddin went to meet Shaukat Hussain Rizvi and said to him, 'Look, you have a rival who is madly in love with your wife and one of these days he is going to run away with her and you will be left watching.' Shaukat asked awkwardly, 'Who is he?' Mian Jalaluddin smiled. 'My grandson.' 'Your grandson! How old is he?' 'About four.' When Nur Jehan heard the story, she declared that she would go and meet her lover and marry him. Shahid Jalal has been in seventh heaven since being given the news and is waiting impatiently for the day when Nur Jehan will come to see him and become his bride.

Recently, someone told me a story about another of Nur Jehan's lovers, who was not four, but a grown-up man, a barber by profession. He would sing her songs all day long and never tire of talking about her. Someone said to him one day, 'Do you really love Nur Jehan?' 'Without doubt,' the barber replied sincerely. 'If you really love her, can you do what the legendary Punjabi lover Mahiwal did for his beloved Sohni? He cut a piece of flesh from his thigh to prove his love,' the man said. The barber gave him his sharp cut-throat razor and said, 'You can take a piece of flesh from any part of my body.' His friend was a strange character because he slashed away a large chunk of flesh from his arm and ran away while the barber fainted after providing this proof of love. When this great lover regained consciousness in Mayo Hospital, Lahore, the first words that came to his lips were, 'Nur Jehan'.

There is a case in court against Nur Jehan these days. She is charged with beating up a young actress by the name of Nighat Sultana. Since it is sub judice, I do not wish to say much as it would amount to contempt of court, but I fail to understand why Nur Jehan beat up this girl. I had never heard of Nighat Sultana before but am told that she comes from East Bengal, from the city of Dhaka. How or when she became an actress, I absolutely have no idea.

Nur Jehan's dashing husband Syed Shaukat Hussain Rizvi is around, as are her lovely children. Then there is the Lahore barber who is prepared to cut himself with a razor to prove his love for her, not to mention her four-year-old lover, Shahid Jalal, also known as Taku, who dreams of making her his bride. And one must not forget those cooks who hang her picture on their kitchen wall and sing her songs in their tuneless voices while washing dishes. And finally, there is Saadat Hasan Manto who cannot stand the sight of her awful brassiere. What beauty she sees in her upturned front bumpers and why Syed Shaukat Hussain Rizvi permits this gross violation of good taste, I am unable to say.

NASEEM: THE FAIRY QUEEN

I had outgrown cinema-going while still in Amritsar. I had seen so many movies that, frankly, they no longer held any fascination for me. That was why, when I arrived in Bombay to edit the weekly *Mussawar*, I stayed away from movie houses altogether for months. Ours was a movie magazine and we could have complimentary tickets for any film we wished to see. The Bombay Talkies production of *Acchut Kanya* had been drawing crowds at a local cinema and I had ignored it, but when it entered its twenty-second week, I became curious. There had to be something there, otherwise why would it run so long, I said to myself.

This was to be my first film show in Bombay. It was also the first time I saw Ashok Kumar and Devika Rani together. Ashok was a bit raw but Devika Rani had given a polished performance. It was a simple story, which had been told in a simple and tasteful manner, free of the usual vulgarity. That started me off and I began to go to the movies with some frequency.

Around this time, an actress by the name of Naseem Bano was beginning to get famous. It was her great beauty which had caught the popular fancy. She was billed as '*pari chehra* Naseem', the fairy-faced one. Her picture was in every paper. She was indeed young and lovely, her most remarkable feature being her large, magnetic eyes. It is the eyes that lend beauty to a woman's face and Naseem Bano had a real good pair.

She had appeared in two movies so far, both produced by Sohrab Modi, and they had been hits but I had not seen them. Why I hadn't, I don't know. Now a new historical film called *Pukar* was being advertised widely by Minerva Movietone with Naseem playing Empress Nur Jahan. Sohrab Modi was set to play an important role as well. The film was a long time in the making, but from the stills that kept appearing in newspapers and magazines it was clear that it was going to be a big production. Naseem looked stunning as the empress.

I was invited to the release. The story was more fiction than history and the presentation was maudlin and rather theatrical. The emphasis appeared to be on dialogues and costumes. While the dialogues were unnatural and dramatized, they were impressively worded and forceful. The effect on the audience was mesmeric. It was the first such film made in India and not only did it become a source of high profits for Sohrab Modi but it brought about a revolution in the movie industry. Naseem's performance was weak, but her great beauty and lovely costumes more than made up for that. I don't recall, but I think after *Pukar*, she made two or three more films, none of which did as well.

There was no dearth of rumours and scandals about her—nothing uncommon in the movie industry. Sometimes it was said that Sohrab Modi was about to marry Naseem, while others maintained that Moazzam Jah, the Nizam of Hyderabad's son, was wooing the actress and would soon make off with her. This was half true because the prince was spending a lot of time in Bombay and had frequently been seen at her Marine Drive home. He spent millions on her and was in some sort of trouble later trying to explain where the money had gone. Money works, and the prince in the end succeeded in persuading Naseem's mother, Shamshad Begum alias Chammiya, to let him win her daughter's attentions. Both women spent some time in Hyderabad as the prince's guests.

However, before long, the worldly-wise Chammiya came to the conclusion that Hyderabad was like a prison, which would stifle her daughter. Whatever she desired by way of comfort was hers to be had but the atmosphere was constricting. And then who knew when the whimsical prince may get bored, leaving Naseem Bano high and dry. It was not easy to get out of the tightly administered Hyderabad state, but Chammiya was a wise and tactful woman and managed to get both herself and her daughter out of there and safely back to Bombay.

When she returned, there was quite a controversy. There were two groups involved in it, one speaking in favour of, and probably on the payroll of, Moazzam Jah, the other made up of Naseem Bano's sympathizers. At one point, they were sticking posters on walls maligning each other. Whatever dirt they had been able to dig up was dug up and splashed across those posters. They must have got tired because, eventually, things quietened down.

By now, I was a full-time movie person, having been engaged as a munshi or scribe by Imperial Film Company at a monthly salary of sixty rupees. I wrote nonsensical dialogues and other gibberish according to the whims of the directors. However, when Seth Nanoobhai Desai of Hindustan Cinetone offered me a hundred rupees, I moved. My first story for the company was called 'Keechar' but it was filmed as *Apni Nagariya*.

One day I read somewhere that a man by the name of Ehsan had set up a new film company called Taj Pictures, the first production of which was going to be *Ujala*, starring pari chehra Naseem. Two famous men were also associated with the company—Kamal Amrohi who had written *Pukar*, and M.A. Mugghani, who was the movie's publicity manager. There was much infighting during the making of *Ujala* between Amrohi, Mugghani and another member of the team, Amir Haider, followed by a court case, but, in the end, they managed to complete the work.

The story was pedestrian, the music weak and the direction lacked spirit, so the film fared badly and Ehsan had to suffer heavy losses, which forced him to shut shop. However, one outcome of this misadventure was that he fell in love with Naseem Bano. She was no stranger to him, because his father, Khan Bahadur Mohammad Suleman, had been her admirer too. Ehsan had therefore known Naseem before his entry into films. During the making of the movie, he got to know her better. Those who observed the two closely said that because of his shy and withdrawn nature Ehsan had been unable to make the kind of impression on Naseem that he wished. On the set, he would go to a corner and just sit there without saying a word, not even talking to her. Whatever his technique, it was successful in the end because we heard one day that the two had got married in Delhi and Naseem had declared that her movie-making days were over.

This was sad news for Naseem's admirers because the great beauty was now to provide joy and comfort to just one man: her husband. How Ehsan and Naseem graduated from courtship to love to actual marriage, I do not know. Ashok Kumar's explanation was the most interesting. One of Ashok's friends, Captain Siddiqi, was closely related to Ehsan and had invested some money in *Ujala*. Ashok used to visit him at his house almost every day but of late he had begun to notice a change in the atmosphere, though he could not put his finger on it. One day he thought he smelt perfume and asked Siddiqi what the source of the fragrance was, but received no reply.

A few days later, Ashok went to Siddiqi's place when he was not in, yet the same old fragrance, light and flirtatious, hung in the air. Ashok went on a reconnaissance of the lower floor, sniffing the air like a hound and came to the conclusion that the source of this delightful odour was upstairs. Quietly, he tiptoed up the stairs and walked into the bedroom, the doors being wide open. What he found was Naseem sprawled on the bed with a man sitting by her side whispering in her ear. Ashok immediately recognized him because he had met him once. It was Ehsan. When Ashok told Captain Siddiqi what he had seen, he smiled. 'This thing has been on for some time,' he conceded.

Ashok's story and the light it sheds on the affair between Ehsan and Naseem needs no commentary. What happened between the two must have been what always happens between lovers. I do know though that Ehsan's mother and his sisters were dead set against the marriage and there were several quarrels in the family on this account. However, the father, Khan Bahadur Mohammad Suleman, had no objection and the marriage went ahead. Naseem left Bombay and moved to Delhi where she had grown up. The newspapers had a field day but then they forgot about it.

During this period, there were many changes in the film world. Several film companies came into being and while some survived, others perished. Many stars were born and quite a few disappeared from the scene. After the tragic death of Himanshu Rai, Bombay Talkies fell into disarray. His wife, Devika Rani, and Rai Bahadur Chunilal, his general manager, quarrelled constantly. There was a break and then Rai Bahadur left Bombay Talkies with his entire group, which included producer S. Mukherjee, director and storywriter Gyan Mukherjee and Ashok Kumar himself. They also took with them the lyricist Kavi Pradeep, sound recordist S. Vacha, comedian V.H. Desai and dialogue writers Shahid Latif and Santoshi. This group set up a new company by the name of Filmistan and S. Mukherjee was appointed production controller. He had already made his mark with a silver jubilee hit and preparations now began for the new outfit's first venture. A story was commissioned, and Mukherjee, still seething because of the old team's treatment at the hands of Devika Rani, made clear his intention of doing something that would make her sit up.

He finally hit upon a plan. He was going to talk Naseem Bano into returning to films. Based on his track record, he was confident that whatever he set his heart on, he would manage to accomplish. He devised a plan to lure Naseem back. Because of Ashok, he had developed good personal relations with Captain Siddiqi. And then wasn't Rai Bahadur Chunilal a good friend of Ehsan's father, the old Khan Bahadur? He approached Ehsan first and though, in the beginning, he was adamant, Mukherjee's persistence paid off and he said 'Yes'. Mukherjee returned to Bombay in triumph and announced to the press that the first Filmistan presentation, *Chal Chal Re Naujawan*, would star Naseem Bano. This created a sensation because it was presumed that Naseem had left the industry permanently.

I had just returned to Bombay after doing a stint lasting a year and a half at All India Radio in Delhi and was busy writing a story for Syed Shaukat Hussain Rizvi. I finished the assignment, wrote a few more stories and during this period hardly left my house. Even my wife got tired of my new domesticity, being convinced that spending so much time indoors was bad for my health. Shahid Latif, whom I had known since my Aligarh days, would drop in to see me whenever his workload at Filmistan permitted him. One day my wife said to him, 'Shahid bhai, I don't like my husband working at home. He is spoiling his health. If he had a job, at least he would be able to get out.' A few days later, Shahid Latif called from Malad saying that Mukherjee wanted to interview me because he was looking for someone for the scenario department.

I wasn't keen on a job, but I went anyway just to take a look at the Filmistan studio. It had a nice atmosphere like that of a university and I was impressed. When I met Mukherjee, I took an immediate liking to him too, and right there and then, I signed a contract. The money was meagre but I felt it might be possible to manage on three hundred rupees a month. I would have to spend an hour travelling to the studio in Goregaon from my residence but I was sure it could be done. One could also make something on the side by moonlighting.

In the beginning, I felt like a stranger in Filmistan, but in a matter of days I got to know everyone and I felt like a part of the family. With Mukherjee I was able to form a friendship, while Naseem Bano I saw only once or twice. As the script was now being written, she would only drop in briefly and then drive back home. Mukherjee was a perfectionist and it was months before he was satisfied with the story. We began to shoot the movie, starting with scenes that did not have Naseem. Then she appeared one day. I found her sitting on a folding chair outside the studio, her legs crossed, drinking tea from a thermos. Ashok introduced us. 'I have read his stories and other pieces,' she said softly.

The conversation was formal and brief. As she was still in make-up, I wasn't sure if she really was beautiful. I felt that when she spoke, she did so with an almost physical effort. There was a world of difference between the Naseem of *Pukar* and that of *Chal Chal Re Naujawan*. While she wore the splendid robes of an empress in the former, she was a uniformed volunteer of the Bharatiya Seva Dal in the latter. After I had seen her thrice without her make-up, I was convinced that she was indeed beautiful. Her mere presence in a room was enough to light up the place, such was her innate natural grace and loveliness.

She dressed with great care and I never saw a woman who had such fine taste in choosing colours. Yellow is a dangerous colour because it can make one look sickly but she wore it in a carefree, cavalier manner, which always startled me. The sari was her favourite, though off and on she would also wear a gharara or shalwar kameez. Even at home she was nicely dressed, being one of those people who take good care of their clothes, which was why even her old ones looked nearly new. I found her to be hard-working and delicate at the same time. She never showed the least sign of fatigue on the set although Mukherjee was a difficult man to please and a scene had to be rehearsed several times before he was satisfied. There she would be under powerful lights, sitting down, getting up, sitting down again, but always without complaint. I learnt later that she loved acting for its own sake. When we looked at the rushes after the day's shooting, her performance would appear lackadaisical. It lacked brilliance. She could enact scenes demanding dignified gestures and her natural good looks were always her greatest advantage, but she could not impress a critical observer who valued the pure art of acting. Her performance in *Chal Chal Re Naujawan* was the best thing she had done until then.

Mukherjee wanted her to give her portrayal an edge but Naseem was by nature a cool and laid-back woman. She could not do it. The day the film was released, there was a party at Taj Hotel. She looked splendid, almost like a Mughal princess, aloof and regal. The movie had taken two years to make, two tiring years, but contrary to expectations, it did not do very well. We were disappointed, especially Mukherjee. However, because of his contract, he was required to oversee the production of another film for Taj Mahal Pictures. He had no option but to get down to work.

Ehsan and Mukherjee had become close friends during the making of *Chal Chal Re Naujawan*. He now wanted him to take complete responsibility for the new production. Mukherjee and I had several meetings and it was decided that I should write a story called *Begum*, which would take full advantage of Naseem's beauty. I prepared a sketch and after some changes made by

Mukherjee we began to shoot the movie, which we were able to complete. When I saw it on the screen, it felt like a vague reflection of what I had written on paper. During the filming of *Begum*, I had frequent opportunities to observe Naseem closely. In fact, Mukherjee and I used to take lunch at her house and often spent our evenings there going over what was to be shot the next day.

I had thought that Naseem would be living in a splendid villa, but when I entered her modest bungalow on Ghodbunder Road, I was taken aback. It was a rundown place with ordinary furniture, which was probably rented. The carpet was worn out and the floors and walls in need of paint. In the middle of this was Naseem, the woman with the face of a fairy, engaged in a discussion with the milkman on the quality of the milk he had just delivered. Her voice, which never seemed to wish to leave her throat, was fully turned on in order to extract a confession from the milkman that he had given her one full pound less than what she was paying for. One pound of undelivered milk! And that complaint from Naseem, for whose sake hundreds of Farhads would have been willing to dig any number of canals flowing with milk! I reeled as the incongruity of the situation hit me.

I found out in the course of time that the Nur Jahan of *Pukar* was a very domestic kind of woman who had every single quality that any run-of-the-mill housewife is supposed to have. When *Begum* went into production, she took charge of the costume department. It was estimated that the costumes would cost ten to twelve thousand rupees, but to save money she had a tailor permanently installed in her house, to whom she gave all her old saris, shirts and ghararas with detailed directions on how to stitch the costumes we would need.

Naseem had lots of clothes and unlike most of us she wore, rather than used, them. The fact was that whatever she wore looked good on her. In *Begum*, Mukherjee had presented her as an artless Kashmiri village damsel. He had also had her wear a Cleopatra-type costume, as well as the long-flowing Punjabi kurta and laacha, and even a modern outfit. It was our belief that *Begum* would be a hit, if for no other reason than for the lovely costumes worn by Naseem. It was a pity that, owing to poor direction and a weak score, the movie did only middling business.

We had all worked very hard, especially Mukherjee. Often we would be up until three in the morning with him putting new touches to the story, and Naseem and Ehsan doing their best to stay awake. As long as Ehsan kept swinging his leg, I knew that he was listening to us, but the moment he stopped, I knew he had gone to sleep. Naseem was always irritated by the fact that her husband could not resist sleep. What was more, he would doze off when we were discussing an important turn in the story. Mukherjee and I would tease Ehsan but Naseem would get upset and try to make him stay awake. However, the more she tried, the sleepier he would become. Finally, Naseem too would begin to show signs of sleepiness and Mukherjee would stand up and leave. I lived quite far from Ghodbunder Road and had to take a train to get home, which I could never manage before midnight. It was sheer torture and we decided after I spoke to Mukherjee that I should move in with Naseem and Ehsan for a few days.

Ehsan was a shy person and would take ages to state what was on his mind. He was keen that I should have every comfort and wanted me to know that I only had to ask for whatever I needed. However, his shyness and innate formality always prevented him from saying this in so many words. Once he asked Naseem to speak to me. 'Whatever you need, just let us know,' she said in the purest Punjabi, which she spoke perfectly. During the filming of *Chal Chal Re Naujawan*, when I told Rafiq Ghaznavi, who was playing an important role in the movie, about Naseem's Punjabi, he said in his typical manner that I was talking rubbish. I tried to convince him that I was serious but without luck.

One day during the shooting, when both Naseem and Rafiq were on the set and Ashok was trying his English tongue-twisters on her, I asked Rafiq, 'Lala, what does *uddhar vanja* mean?' 'What language is that?' he wanted to know. 'Punjabi,' I answered. 'I don't know,' Rafiq said, adding, 'you son of an *uddhar vanja*.' Naseem arched her neck slightly, smiled at Rafiq and asked in Punjabi, 'You really don't know?' When Rafiq heard Naseem

speaking Punjabi, he forgot his Pushto. After the initial shock
had passed, he asked her in halting Urdu, 'You know Punjabi?'
Naseem kept smiling. 'Yes.' 'Then you tell me what *uddhar vanja*
means,' I butted in. She thought for a few seconds, then said,
'*Uddhar vanja* means the clothes you put on when you want
to get comfortable at home and are not expecting any visitors.'
Rafiq Ghaznavi forgot what little Pushto he still remembered.

Naseem's grandmother was a Kashmiri from Amritsar, which
was how she had learnt Punjabi. Urdu she spoke with great purity
because she had grown up in Delhi where her mother lived.
English she knew because she had been sent to a school run by
nuns. She was fond of music because of her mother, but she did
not have her sweet voice, and although she sang her own songs
in the movies in which she acted, her voice lacked richness. She
later stopped singing altogether.

The halo around Naseem had gradually disappeared for me.
What did it for me was the bath I took at their place. I expected
the bathroom to be well equipped, with a variety of bath salts,
exotic soaps and a whole range of toiletries that actresses and
women who care about their looks use to look more beautiful.
But all it had was a metal bucket, an aluminium utensil to pour
water from and heavy water from a Malad well that refused
to let any lather form no matter how long and hard one tried.

As for Naseem, whenever you saw her, she invariably looked
fresh and lovely. Her make-up was worn light. She hated deep
colours, preferring pastel shades, which were in line with her
cool, laid-back personality. She loved perfumes and had a whole
range of them, some both rare and expensive. She had heaps
of ornaments but you would never see her weighed down with
them. Perhaps a bracelet with a diamond sometimes, or a couple
of gold bangles or maybe just a pearl necklace. That was all.

Her table was equally simple. Ehsan had asthma and Naseem
always seemed to have a cold, so they were careful about what
they ate. Naseem would remove the green chillies from my plate
and Ehsan would pick out food from hers. They would have light
arguments over their meals, but when you caught them looking
at each other you detected love.

Once my wife invited Naseem to the house for dinner. She loved the ghee we used to cook our curries with and asked my wife, 'Where do you get this?' 'From the store. It is made by Polson. It is sold everywhere,' my wife answered. 'Could you get me two tins?' Naseem asked. I told the servant to run across the road and get two tins since I had an account at my neighbourhood grocery store. Over the next few months we purchased eight tins for her. One day she said to me, 'We should settle that ghee account.' 'There is no need,' I answered, but when she insisted, I said, 'In all there were eight tins. You can work out the cost.' Naseem was silent for a few minutes then said, 'Eight? Maybe there were seven.' 'Maybe there were seven,' I replied. 'Why maybe? If you say there were eight, then there must have been eight,' she said. 'Well you too said "maybe",' I told her. She kept going over this seven-eight business for a long time. She was sure there had been only seven. The store from where they had been purchased said there were eight, as did I. The only way this could be settled was if one of us accepted the other's figure; but since it was a question of accounts, neither side was willing to give in. Finally, Naseem asked her servant to bring out the empty tins. There were only seven of them. She looked at me triumphantly. 'You can count them . . . seven.' 'There may be seven,' I replied, 'but according to my count, there were eight.' At this point, the servant spoke, 'Yes, there were eight but the sweeper woman took one.'

I was paid five hundred rupees a month and had to account for every single paisa, but we never had any problem. Both husband and wife were happy with my work, though Ehsan was somewhat uneasy with my impatient temperament, but since he was extremely formal, he could never bring himself to say it. Outwardly, Ehsan was a weak person but he was firm with his wife. Naseem was only allowed to socialize with certain people and they did not include most actors and actresses. Naseem herself did not care for superficial types, nor had she any patience with noisy or raucous parties. Let me narrate the story of one in which she figured.

This happened at Holi. Like the 'mud-slinging party' at

the Aligarh University at the start of the monsoon season, the tradition at Bombay Talkies was a Holi party. Since almost everyone at Filmistan was a former Bombay Talkies person, the tradition had been continued.

Mukherjee was the ringleader at the colour-throwers' party, while the women were under the command of his plump and good-humoured wife, who happened to be Ashok Kumar's sister. I was at Shahid Lateef's house, and his wife, Ismat Chughtai, and my wife, Safia, were busy gossiping when we heard a noise outside. 'There they are, Safia,' Ismat said. It was the Holi party indeed. Ismat was insistent that no one sprinkle any coloured water on her. I was afraid this would lead to unpleasantness since the merrymakers were in a holiday mood. Luckily, she soon relented and was drenched in colour within minutes. Shahid and I were in the same condition; in fact we all looked like multi-coloured goblins. Some more people joined us. Suddenly, Shahid shouted, 'On to pari chehra Naseem's house.'

Armed with coloured water in buckets and syringes, our raucous band ran down Ghodbunder Road towards Naseem's house and arrived there within minutes. They were both home. Naseem, perfectly made-up, was wearing a lovely, soft-coloured georgette sari. 'Go for them!' Shahid ordered, but I suggested that we give them time to change. Naseem smiled. 'I am all right the way I am.' The words were hardly out of her mouth when she was drenched in coloured water from every direction. Within seconds, she had been transformed into an evil-looking witch. The whites of her eyes and her sparkling teeth looked most odd in her multicoloured face, as if a child had upturned a bottle of ink on a painting by Behzad or Monet.

After we were done with this, a kabbadi match began. The men played first, the women followed. Whenever Mukherjee's plump wife fell to the ground, there was much laughter all around. Since my wife wore glasses, she was unable to see much and would run in the wrong direction. Naseem could not run because she wasn't used to this kind of horseplay. However, she was into the spirit of the thing and took part in everything enthusiastically.

Naseem and her husband were deeply religious, the kind who reverently kiss and touch their eyes with bits of old Urdu newspapers they pick up from the ground, fearing that the holy words printed on them may otherwise be desecrated. If they see a single star in the sky as the evening falls, they search for a group of nine and a pair for luck. You had to see Ehsan at the race course to believe how superstitious he was. If a one-eyed man were to stand next to him, he would have dropped dead. If a horse on which he had a tip but on which he had not bet, won, he would fight with Naseem. 'Why did you tell me not to back that horse?' But such arguments are a part of any marriage.

Naseem's two children were always at their grandmother's because she wanted them to stay away from film studios. She had loved her late father intensely and always kept his picture in her vanity bag. I have a strange fascination with women's bags and the bric-a-brac they contain. One day I was looking through the bag that she had left lying around when she suddenly appeared. 'I am sorry. I am indulging a bad old habit of mine,' I explained, adding, 'but tell me whose picture that is.' Naseem took the picture from my hand, gazed at it longingly and said, 'My Abbu's, who else's?' I felt that she was a little girl who was proudly showing me what her father looked like. I did not ask her what he was or where he now was. Was it not enough that he was her father . . . no, her Abbu.

One night, during the writing of the movie *Begum*, it got very late as Mukherjee and I had got involved in a long discussion on some aspects of the screenplay. It was almost two in the morning and the first local train would not leave until 3.30 a.m. My wife was with me. When we wanted to leave, Naseem said, 'No, Safia, this is no time to go. Stay here.' We said we would rather go because the weather was nice and we would walk up and down on the platform till the train arrived. But both Naseem and Ehsan were insistent that we stay on. Mukherjee left as he had a car and did not have far to go. I slept on the veranda and Ehsan lay down on a sofa in the living room. When we left after breakfast, Safia told me an interesting story.

When Naseem and she entered the bedroom, she found only

one bed there. 'Why don't you take it?' my wife suggested. Naseem smiled, laid out a fresh sheet and said, 'But let us change first.' Then she gave Safia one of her new sleeping suits to wear, assuring her that it was 'absolutely new'. Safia put it on and lay down. Naseem changed languidly and then removed her make-up. Safia said she was taken aback. 'Naseem, how pale you are!' she exclaimed. A faint smile appeared on Naseem's unpainted lips. Then she rubbed her face with various ointments, washed her hands and picked up the Quran and began to recite from it. 'Naseem, I swear you are so much better than people like us,' Safia said. Then she suddenly realized that this had not been a tactful remark, and fell silent. Naseem finished her recitation and promptly went to sleep.

This was Naseem, the woman with the face of a goddess . . . the Nur Jahan of the movie *Pukar* . . . the Queen of Beauty . . . Ehsan's Roshan (his name for her) . . . Chammiya's daughter and mother of two children.